Living Beyond the Ordinary

Developing an Extraordinary Relationship With God

Tom Kraeuter

Emerald Books

P.O. Box 635
Lynnwood, WA 98046

Training Resources
Hillsboro, Missouri

Emerald Books are distributed through YWAM Publishing. For a full list of titles, including other books by Tom Kraeuter, visit our website at: www.ywampublishing.com

Published by Emerald Books
P.O. Box 635
Lynnwood, WA 98046

ISBN 1-883002-71-0

All Scripture quotations are from either the King James Version or The Holy Bible, New International Version, copyright © 1973, 1978, 1984 International Bible Society. Used by permission of Zondervan Bible Publishers.

Printed in the United States of America.

Other books by Tom Kraeuter

If Standing Together Is So Great,
Why Do We Keep Falling Apart?
Real Answers to Walking in Unity

Worship Is...What?!
Rethinking Our Ideas About Worship

The Worship Leader's Handbook

Keys to Becoming
an Effective Worship Leader

Developing an Effective Worship Ministry

Things They Didn't Teach Me
in Worship Leading School

More Things They Didn't Teach Me
in Worship Leading School

I humbly dedicate this book to
my wonderful children,
David, Stephen and Amy.

As a father, I long for you to learn
the most important lessons of life.
The lessons in this book are the ones
I pray most earnestly
will be instilled in you.

$\mathcal{T}$hanks to:

Nick Ittzes, my pastor and my friend.
Nick, without your profound teaching and
mentoring this book would never have been written.

Others who have greatly influenced my teaching,
including the late Dr. Bob Heil, Judson Cornwall,
Kent Henry, and R.C. Sproul.

Jennifer Brody, not only for fixing my grammatical errors (and they were
many) but for asking the thought-provoking questions.
Jenn, your analytical thinking made this a much better book than it
would have been without you.

Diane Lopez for the initial meticulous proofreading.

Allebach Creative Associates, Inc., Souderton, Pennsylvania,
for a great cover design.

Those who reviewed the manuscript ahead of time.

Special thanks to my wonderful wife,
Barbara, my faithful encourager and supporter.
Barb, you're the best!

WARNING:

This book may change the way you live!

If you are 100% satisfied with your life and your relationship
with God, then close this book now.
Otherwise, get ready for an adventure that could
radically alter your life.

$\mathscr{C}$ONTENTS

ntroduction

Augustine said of God, "You have made us for Yourself, and our hearts are restless until they find their rest in You." Our relationship with God is the key that makes everything else in life make sense.

So, based on the title of this book, what exactly is an *extraordinary* relationship with the Lord? I took an informal survey while working on this book and found that most people equate "extraordinary" with ideas like "exciting," "thrilling," and "sensational." Although there may be a dimension of that excitement involved, the true definition of extraordinary is simply "beyond ordinary." That's the real goal: that we are moving forward, not becoming stagnant. True Christianity is not achieving some particular level, a plateau, and staying there. Unfortunately, that is the ordinary scenario. Real life in Christ is meant to be a progressive forward movement in our relationship with the Lord.

This book has taken me a long time to complete. Several times I was certain it was finished, and each time there was a delay in publishing it. When that happened I added to and adjusted what I had already written. One day during this process I was with a group of people and asked them to pray for me to be able to finish the book the way God wanted it to be done. I said, "I keep having this recurring sense that each delay has been orchestrated by God because what I thought was the finished product was really not yet finished. I want it to be thorough enough that I don't have to look back a year from now and say, 'Oh, I wish I would have added this or that.'"

> ...the true definition of extraordinary is simply "beyond ordinary." That's the real goal: that we are moving forward, not becoming stagnant.

As the group prayed for me, a young lady—obviously the youngest of the group—said, "God, I pray that Tom will want to change it in a year." My initial reaction was, "She's got a lot of nerve!" Then I realized she was right. If indeed our relationship with God is progressive, then a year from now I should be more mature and have more insight. That should be true for all of us.

My experience has been that Christians long for a progressively closer walk with the Lord but often fall short. There can be many underlying reasons for this (some of which we will address in this book), but one common reason is simply a lack of understanding. We often do not understand how to relate to God, what is involved in such a relationship, or even why He wants a relationship with us.

Once we begin to understand the relationship, then old patterns of the unfulfilling relationship need to be replaced with new ones.

The practical concepts in this book will help you do just that. Each chapter is designed to be read and meditated upon. There is a personal application section at the end of each chapter to assist you in reflecting on the material.

The natural tendency is to simply read this book straight through. However, to receive the full benefit, it is imperative that you consider the personal application questions. These questions are designed to help you apply the theme of the chapter to *your* life. It would be best to carefully read and consider each question and even write out applicable answers. You might even consider keeping a journal of your thoughts as you proceed.

Please realize that this is not meant to be a book that causes you to marvel at the wisdom of one who has "arrived." Far from it. I am simply a fellow-pilgrim who wants the fullest possible relationship with God. Some days are better than others in accomplishing this in my own life. However, when I remember and practice the principles in this book, I see a marked difference in how I relate to my Creator.

Let us—you and me together—learn and grow as we consider how we can live beyond the ordinary and, indeed, have an extraordinary relationship with God.

Part 1

The Priority of Relationship

Chapter 1

God's Priority: Relationship

uppose I was given a 1957 Chevy. For the most part the car is in good shape, but I decide it could use a bit of work. For instance, the interior isn't as fashionable as I would like, so I choose to replace it with the interior from a brand-new Cadillac. Hey, that's much nicer! Now, those fins on the back...they could hurt someone. I'll just cut those off and make the rear fenders round and smooth. And that gas-guzzling engine has got to go. A nice, little, up-to-date 4-cylinder job will be much more economical. Add some ultramodern, electric-blue paint and it's done. Wha'd'ya think?

If you are an automobile buff, you are probably gagging. You may even be thinking that with all those changes the car is really no longer a '57 Chevy. Well, it is...but it isn't.

Now suppose one of Jesus' original disciples was somehow transported to present-day North America. If he looked at the Church as a whole, would he have the same response? "I recognize a few things, but some of the modifications have compromised the basic design."

When Jesus was asked about what He considered to be the most important thing, He responded, "Love the Lord your God with all your heart and with all your soul and with all your mind" (Matthew 22:38). Jesus stripped away all the extras and focused on what was really important: our relationship with God. From Jesus' perspective, all the other things are just peripherals.

An honest evaluation of Scripture will point to one inescapable conclusion: God wants relationship with His people. To miss this point would be to miss the very essence of the Bible.

Ultimately, our fellowship with God is the reason Jesus went to the cross. The Lord redeemed us so that we might once again be in right relationship with Him. Far more than our selfish ideas of eternal fire insurance, God's goal is fellowship. When everything is over, when time as we know it comes to an end, what does our Creator/Redeemer get for all His work? It's us. You and me. We are the final prize. Our relationship with Him is what God is after.

It should be understood that when I refer to relationship with God, I'm not talking about just a saving relationship. You may be headed for heaven, but do you have a real, honest, dynamic relationship with God here and now? The Lord is not so much interested in simply saving us from hell but in establishing an intimate, interactive, day-by-day relationship with Him.

"Here I am! I stand at the door and knock. If anyone hears My voice and opens the door, I will come in and eat with him, and he with Me" (Revelation 3:20). These words of Jesus are often used for evangelistic purposes. However, evangelism was not the original context. This statement was part of a wake-up call to the Laodicean

Church. Their faith had become lukewarm. They had forgotten how desperately they needed God. However, they were still Christians. This was not a message to heathen, but to God's people. What He is saying is, "I want to fellowship with you, My people."

Ultimately Christianity is not about going to church. It is not even so much about heaven and hell. It is about an active relationship with God.

The Lord is so totally self-sufficient that He really does not need anything. If that's true, then what is it that He wants from us? We often think He wants our service, so we seek to serve and serve and serve. Or we think He wants money—so we give. However, God, Who owns the cattle on a thousand hills and created every living creature, has the ability and resources to accomplish His will so much better than we ever could. So what is He really looking for? True relationship.

> **Ultimately Christianity is not about going to church. It is not even so much about heaven and hell. It is about an active relationship with God.**

In her book *Ministering to God*, Victoria Brooks said it like this:

> We are surrounded by relationships, but driven by accomplishment. God is the opposite. Though surrounded by His accomplishments, He has given Himself to relationship. Though not in need of interaction, He has chosen to pursue it. For God, fellowship is the goal.[1]

From the wording of Genesis 3:8 we get the impression that the Lord walking in the garden of Eden "in the cool of the day" was a normal occurrence. Of course we know that God is a Spirit and therefore does not have a physical body. But Scripture often refers to God as having physical attributes. This helps us understand Him better. Did He actually take on human characteristics to walk in the garden? We don't know for certain, but there was obviously some deeper level of fellowship going on before the fall into sin than we know and experience today.

In light of this, what do you suppose happened in God's heart when Adam and Eve sinned? It was not just the sin itself that caused God grief. Please understand that sin is heinous in the sight of

God—He hates sin! Yet, sin was not the main issue. The real problem was the result of the sin: the breaking of fellowship. God desired relationship, and Adam and Eve broke it off.

In the Gospel of John, Jesus said, "Yet a time is coming and has now come when the true worshipers will worship the Father in spirit and truth, for *they are the kind of worshipers the Father seeks*" (John 4:23, author's emphasis). The Greek word for "seeks" in this verse conveys the meaning of the Lord actually searching for something. There are not many places where the Bible refers to God searching for something. So when we find a passage that suggests Him looking—hunting, if you will—then we should pay special attention to it. This verse says that the Father is seeking worshipers. He is looking for those who will enter into an intimate love relationship with Him. Dynamic (as opposed to static) relationship is God's priority.

We need to recognize that priority. Just as He did with Adam and Eve, and as He did with the Laodicean Church, God desires fellowship with us. Throughout the Bible it is obvious that the Lord's supreme goal is to be in true relationship with His people.

Personal application:

1. Have you understood (before this) how much priority God places on relationship? Search for other examples in Scripture of how much He desires fellowship with us.

2. What does the phrase "personal relationship with God" mean to you? Is your relationship with God a personal one?

3. What one tangible thing could you do today that would indicate that you want to make relationship with God as important to you as it is to Him?

$\mathscr{P}$riorities: Lip Service or Real Life?

$\mathscr{R}$ecently I have been giving a lot of serious consideration to my priorities—what's really important? I have a friend who is a management consultant. If I want to be challenged about how and why I'm doing certain things in ministry, I only need to spend an hour or so with him. He asks the hard questions. He doesn't mince words. He consistently makes a beeline for the heart of the matter. I hate those conversations. Yet, at the same time, I love them.

A periodic assessment of our priorities is absolutely vital. Businesses today do this regularly, and they are ruthless in making certain that their stated goals are happening. Whatever may get in the way of those priorities—a money-grabbing program, a time-wasting item, an energy-sapping event—these and more are unquestioningly cut so that the real priorities can be accomplished.

> **A periodic assessment of our priorities is absolutely vital. Businesses today do this regularly, and they are ruthless in making certain that their stated goals are happening.**

Please realize that these things may not be easy to cut. Some of these items may have been around for a long time, and it may have heart-wrenching effects to cut them. However, in order to meet the true goals, the items that hinder that from occurring must go. Are there things in your life that need to be cut out?

In Acts 6 the Church was growing, and the demands on the time of the apostles were also growing. Finally they were forced to reevaluate their priorities. They not only reevaluated, but they took steps to achieve those priorities. They said, "...we will give our attention to..." and they stated their priorities. Another translation puts it this way: "We will give our best energies to..." What is it that you give your "best energies" to?

Without an honest evaluation of our lives, at least periodically, it is easy for us to become mired in the peripheral issues. We can begin to major on the minors and minor on the majors. Let me explain.

It is obvious from both Scripture and experience that God's original design for the Church has one top priority: knowing Him. Our relationship to the Lord is the key that makes all the rest of life work. Unfortunately, it is also the area where much of the Church is willing to compromise. We too often spend far more time doing the work of the Church and miss the relationship that the Lord desires to have with us. In order to fully function as the Church God wants us to be, knowing Him is vital.

Throughout this book we will explore in detail the whole issue of being in proper biblical relationship with the Lord. I have made an effort to strip away the peripheral issues and concentrate solely on this one priority.

I have been told that sometimes I am a bit too candid in my teaching. People feel somewhat uncomfortable when a teacher is obviously human. As human beings, we tend to want to learn from someone we can put on a pedestal, not someone who struggles as we do. At the risk of being too candid, let's be brutally honest for a moment. Are you always 100% satisfied with your relationship with God? I didn't think so. Neither am I. All too frequently I pursue everything but the one thing that I know is most important in my life. In doing that, I have missed the relationship that God wants me to have with Him.

Dr. Donald, in his book *The Trivialization of God*, phrased it like this:

> It is worth noting that God gave the commandment against other gods not to pagans but to Israel, the very people of God. Being saved never guarantees worship of the true God. God can seem too distant, too slow in appearing, too unaccommodating to individual desires. The consequent longings easily seduce into adulterous liaisons with more immediately satisfying gods. But when the afternoon's diversion has passed, unfulfillment comes raging back with even greater intensity. By then, though, the marriage has been defiled, the God of salvation has been betrayed.[1]

He's right. How many times have I committed spiritual adultery? How many times have I pursued anything and everything but my relationship with the Lord? And what about you? Are you any different? We must begin to recognize that our number one priority in life—the key that causes everything else to work—is our relationship with the Lord.

My family and I live out in the country. A couple years ago some folks built a new home near us. In the process they put in a long, uphill gravel driveway. When the grading was being done for the driveway, a sizeable amount of dirt was removed near the base of a huge old oak tree. Over time, when it rained, more of the dirt around the base washed away. Last summer a torrential wind storm blew through our area, and that old tree toppled over. It hadn't rotted out and died. The foundation had eroded.

I have seen that same erosion happen in the lives of believers more times than I care to recall. As a result of living in a very Godless society, foundations begin to erode. If your spiritual foundation is not consistently shored up, it can erode also. If we do nothing to maintain and build our relationship with God, it will soon wither and fade.

In his book *Life Lessons*, Robert C. Savage made a very strong statement: "Most people are willing to pay more to be amused than to be educated." As I travel coast to coast, I find this to be all too true. We are too often far more willing to spend time and money on leisure, unenduring pursuits, than we are on our spiritual life. What a sad commentary on our society.

> **How many times have I committed spiritual adultery? How many times have I pursued anything and everything but my relationship with the Lord?**

As Christians we must stop giving lip service to "priorities" and instead live those priorities. If it means the house is a little messier than you would like it, it is worth it. If it means that you make less money because you work fewer hours, the trade-off is more than adequate.

If we are truly to be the people of God that the Bible describes, then it will cost something: our lives. If you are not certain you're ready to pay such a price, let me assure you that the eternal benefits more than outweigh any momentary inconvenience. This book will offer practical thoughts on how to cultivate a close, intimate relationship with God. And through it the Holy Spirit may just revolutionize *your* heart and life!

Personal application:

What are your priorities right now? How we spend our time and money are good practical indicators of what is really important to us.

1. Look at your checkbook record for the last month. Break your expenditures into several major categories (i.e., housing/utilities, auto/transportation, char-

itable giving/tithing, recreation, personal development, miscellaneous, etc.). What does this tell you about your priorities?

2. Record how you spend the hours in a "normal" week. Categorize your various activities (i.e., sleep, hygiene, work, travel, recreation/leisure, fitness, prayer/ Bible study, church, miscellaneous, etc.). What does this tell you about your real priorities?

3. Based on your answers to the first two questions, what one thing should you consider changing to make your relationship with God a top priority?

$\mathcal{D}$addy...

$\mathcal{S}$o what does our relationship with God look like? What form should this relationship take?

People often express their true feelings at times of strong emotion. We weep for a loved one at the side of a casket as emotions are loosed and true feelings surface. Tears of joy flow over the recovery of a stricken family member because that which is real on the inside is being let out in true emotion. In this sense, Jesus was the same as we. When He was at a point of strong emotion, His deepest inner feelings came forth and became more evident than usual.

"O Jerusalem, Jerusalem, you who kill the prophets and stone those sent to you, how often I have longed to gather your children together, as a hen gathers her chicks under her wings, but you were not willing!" (Luke 13:34). You can almost hear the yearning in His voice. It is the sound of a loving parent lamenting over the wayward child.

> **As we mature, the ever-increasing responsibilities of life tend to strip away our innocence and simplicity. But increased reliance on God helps bring them back.**

The night before His crucifixion Jesus displayed intense emotion in the Garden of Gethsemane. He called out, "Abba, Father..." (Mark 14:36). In essence the word "Abba" means "Daddy." According to a Rabbinical commentary on the traditional teaching of the Jews, slaves were forbidden to address the head of the family by this title. It was apparently a more personal, more intimate word. In His most trying hour, Jesus called God, "Daddy." The only other two times "Abba" is used in Scripture are in the context of believers using that word. Romans 8:15 and Galatians 4:6 both tell us that we can call God "Daddy" because we are no longer slaves but sons. We are His children, and He is our loving heavenly Father.

In the Bible, "Abba" is always used in conjunction with the word "Father." *Vines Expository of New Testament Words* says this, "'Abba' is the word framed by the lips of infants, and betokens unreasoning trust; 'father' expresses an intelligent apprehension of the relationship. The two together express the love and intelligent confidence of the child."1

Do you ever long for a few moments of childhood again? Do you ever desire to return to the innocence and simplicity, a time of no concerns about the future and no regrets about the past? Do you ever think about a time when you were a child and wish it could be like that again?

In the book *Away With the Manger: A Spiritually Correct Christmas*, one of the characters was reluctantly looking forward to

Christmas and the gift he would receive. At one point he wishes, "Just once, just one Christmas, may it not be a tie. Or a sweater. Or a book that someone else wanted to read—someone who hopes you'll leave it lying around so they can pick it up. Just once let it be something that makes me feel like a child again."[2]

Nearly all of us long to feel like a child again. We want to experience again the innocence and simplicity of that now long ago period of time. A time when there was no need to worry about the myriad of things that now press in on us every day. A time when we were less concerned about how our life would ultimately play out here on earth. We all desire to recapture that innocence and simplicity of childhood. But we never will, at least not fully. We cannot go back. There is, however, at least a dimension of that innocence and simplicity found in the Kingdom of God. That's why Jesus told us that we must become like children (Luke 18:17).

As we mature, the ever-increasing responsibilities of life tend to strip away our innocence and simplicity. But increased reliance on God helps bring them back. Jesus said: "Come to Me, all you who are weary and burdened, and I will give you rest. Take My yoke upon you and learn from Me, for I am gentle and humble in heart, and you will find rest for your souls. For My yoke is easy and My burden is light" (Matthew 11:28-30).

When we fully trust God—when we can climb up on Daddy's lap and know that regardless of the situation everything is just fine—we become less weary and less burdened. True relationship with the Lord recaptures a dimension of that long-ago innocence and simplicity of childhood.

Please realize that I am aware that some people have had a less than desirable childhood. Perhaps there was a father who had no time to be daddy. Or maybe he was physically or verbally abusive. Or perhaps there was no father present at all. All of these unfortunate situations can implant a misunderstanding of our heavenly Father. However, the truth is that none of us had a perfect childhood. All of our earthly fathers were flawed. Each of us, though, has some mental picture of an ideal father. That ideal father—and much more—is what God wants to be to us.

The relationship that the Lord—our "Abba, Father"—wants us to have with Him is the innocent, unreasoning trust of a child, as well as the intellectual comprehension toward a loving parent who always wants what is best for us.

Personal application:

1. In your most trying hours, do you call God, "Daddy!" and talk with Him about what is going on? If yes, when was a significant time in your life when you remember running to "Daddy"? If no, why not?

2. List the qualities you think make an ideal Father. (If you're really ambitious, find Scriptures that describe God in this way.)

3. Make this your prayer:
"Heavenly Father—Daddy—in a world where everything so often seems to be falling apart, I trust You. Today I choose to climb up in Your lap and know that You are still in control and that I have nothing to fear or worry about because You are my true, loving Father and I am Your child. Teach me how to have the kind of relationship with You that You truly want me to have. I thank You that You hear me and will answer." Now just spend some time talking to your heavenly Father in your own words.

ellowship With God

The eleventh chapter of Hebrews has been referred to as the "hall of faith." The star players of the Old Testament are there. Noah is mentioned. Abraham is there along with Isaac and Jacob. Moses receives a deservedly lengthy section. Included, of course, are the likes of Gideon and Samson, David and Samuel. Nearly all the Old Testament heroes of the faith are there. One of the first names on the list is a guy named Enoch. Please excuse my apparent disrespect, but I'm not sure that Enoch belongs on the same list with folks like Noah, David, and Abraham. After all, we know who David was: arguably the greatest king in the history of Israel. Abraham has become known as the father of the faithful. Noah spent years building the ark in obedience to God. Moses led the people of Israel out of Egypt and through the desert for forty years. These guys did stuff that you or I would be proud to say we had done. Each one of these folks is what legends are made of. There is no doubt that they should be on the list. But Enoch? Who is he?

The thought of hand-to-hand combat with Philistine warriors scares me, but I can walk with God.

Consider this: his entire life story is summed up in the span of just seven short verses (Genesis 5:18-24). Scripture does not give much background on Enoch at all. We don't even know if he was a stonemason, a woodcutter, a preacher, or an unemployed homeless person. But we do know this: he had pleased God (Hebrews 11:5). How did he do that? He "walked with God" (Genesis 5:24).

There's hope in that statement for you and me. You see, I'm uncertain about what I would do if the Lord asked me to lead His people into battle. Or build an ark. Or rule over His people. These and the other feats of the heroes of the faith seem overwhelming to me. But I can walk with God. I may not know much about parting seas, but I can walk with God. The thought of hand-to-hand combat with Philistine warriors scares me, but I can walk with God. You and I may be intimidated by the idea of doing great exploits in the name of Jesus, but we can walk with God. More than all the great accomplishments that you or I will ever achieve, walking with God—being in honest relationship with Him—is the most important.

So what does it really mean to have a relationship with God? Unquestionably it takes a great deal of effort to build a good relationship. It also takes much time.

When I teach about building a relationship with God at various churches, I often ask how many of the people consider themselves an acquaintance of the pastor—they've met him or perhaps talked in passing. Usually, most of the people in the service will raise their hands. Then I ask how many would consider themselves a friend of the pastor—they have spent time together, maybe been at his house or he at theirs. With this question there is usually a significant drop in the number of raised hands, although most times there are still quite a few. Then I ask one last question. "How many consider yourself a close friend of the pastor? You know what he likes and dislikes. You know why he acts as he does. You are a close friend." At this point there are very seldom more than just a few hands that go up.

I explain that the reason the numbers went down with each successive question is simply because of time spent together. Relationship with anyone involves spending time together. The more time spent, generally the closer the relationship. The same is true for our relationship with God. We will never have a close, intimate knowing of our Lord unless we take the necessary time to cultivate that relationship.

There are numerous aspects that make up a solid relationship between two people. There are times of great intimacy. There are times of making requests of each other. But there are also other times when you are just friends—no great lightning bolts out of the sky, no earth-shaking excitement, just being friends.   Times like this can be nothing more than sitting together on the porch. At other times it could mean talking about the weather. Sometimes it may mean watching a movie together. Not the stuff of great depth but still a very important part of building friendships.   We need these times with God, too. The Lord wants to be included in our everyday lives *as a friend.*

While this is true, we also need times that are more disciplined, set apart just for God, to develop and maintain our relationship with Him. This concept is similar to a marriage relationship. Although much time in a marriage is spent together with the children and others, it is still essential for the husband and wife to spend time alone together. The relationship needs those times to become stronger. Likewise, we too need one-on-one time with our Lord.

You may have seen witnessing tools that suggest man has a God-shaped hole inside. The idea being put forth is that only by inviting Jesus into your heart can the void be filled. In reality, that's only part of the story. Many people invite the Lord in and then ignore Him. That will leave just as much of a void. We need fellowship with God.

From the point of salvation, our entire Christian walk must be a deepening of our fellowship with God. Just as in our human relationships it is essential that we take time to cultivate friendships, the same is true in our relationship with the Lord. It will take time to strengthen that relationship, but it will always be time well spent.

Personal application:

1. *How close would you say you and God are?*
    Acquaintance   Friend   Close Friend

2. *What are the different ways you spend time with God?*

3. *What is one way you might spend more time with God to deepen your friendship/relationship?*

Chapter 5

$\mathscr{O}$ur First Priority

$\mathscr{I}$n the thirty-third chapter of Exodus, God is rather upset with
Israel.

> Then the LORD said to Moses, "Leave this place, you and the peo-
> ple you brought up out of Egypt, and go up to the land I prom-
> ised on oath to Abraham, Isaac and Jacob, saying, 'I will give it
> to your descendants.' I will send an angel before you and drive

out the Canaanites, Amorites, Hittites, Perizzites, Hivites and Jebusites. Go up to the land flowing with milk and honey. But I will not go with you, because you are a stiff-necked people and I might destroy you on the way" (Exodus 33:1-3).

If you understand the context, this is an amazing statement. God had brought the Israelites out of Egypt, promising them that He was going to take them into a "land flowing with milk and honey." That Promised Land had become their dream, their goal, their vision. They could almost taste the flavor of the milk and honey. Possessing that land was their driving force. Then came the incident with the golden calf, and God became angry with the people.

The section of Scripture above follows right after the golden calf scenario. I find it amazing that following such a despicable act the Lord still offers to give them their dream. He tells them that He will send an angel into the land to destroy the present inhabitants. They could then take possession of their awaited Promised Land. But God refuses to go with them. In essence, the Lord is saying, "You can have the land that you long for, but you can't have Me."

Fortunately, Moses has a strong enough relationship with God as well as the presence of mind to intercede and cause God to change His mind. Finally, God relents and agrees to go with them. Moses says: "If Your Presence does not go with us, do not send us up from here" (Exodus 33:15).

The essence of what Moses is saying in these words is, "God, I would rather perish here in the desert with You than to go on and see my dream fulfilled without You." The goal of the Promised Land was good. It was from God. But without Him, it had absolutely no meaning for Moses.

It's not that Moses relished the idea of staying in the desert. Nor was he necessarily excited about fighting the inhabitants of the Promised Land. All of those details, important as they were, paled in comparison when Moses considered the possibility of severing his relationship with God.

Luke, the physician, relates the following story:

As Jesus and His disciples were on their way, He came to a village where a woman named Martha opened her home to Him. She had a sister called Mary, who sat at the Lord's feet listening

to what He said. But Martha was distracted by all the preparations that had to be made.

She came to Him and asked, "Lord, don't you care that my
sister has left me to do the work by myself? Tell her to help me!"

"Martha, Martha," the Lord answered, "you are worried and
upset about many things, but only one thing is needed. Mary
has chosen what is better, and it will not be taken away from
her" (Luke 10:38-42).

My family is part of a home fellowship group at our church. We
meet regularly for prayer and encouragement in a small group context. Some time ago in this group we were looking at this section of
Scripture from Luke. After reading these verses, the leader of the
group asked, "Which of these two women do you identify with the
most?" I carefully avoided eye contact with him because I really was
not interested in answering that question. Would you like to answer
it?

Jesus' words in this passage are very convicting to me: "...only
one thing is needed." Martha was busy doing lots of good things.
The house was probably spotless and she was very likely preparing a
meal that was a culinary work of art. But Mary chose to sit at the
feet of Jesus. And it was Mary who received the commendation from
the Master.

In his book *One Thing Needful*, Gary Mathena said it like this:

Martha could not believe that Mary could be so thoughtless as
to leave her with all the meal preparations. Martha, busy "serving Christ," thinks she has grounds to be angry with her lazy
sister, and even chides Jesus for allowing the injustice to continue. How surprised Martha must have been when Jesus
sweetly and lovingly began to rebuke her: "Martha, Martha,
thou art careful and troubled about many things." As many as
Christ loves, He chastens; and He certainly loved Martha. He
told her that all the fussing and fretting over making the meal
was good, but there was really only one thing needful, and that
was to sit at His feet and learn of Him. All the meetings
attended, all the Christian work done, all the organizations
administered, all the things we do in service to Christ is good
and fine, but we must constantly remind ourselves that there is

only one thing needful, and that is to commune with Him in adoration and worship.[1]

I am not suggesting that we abandon everything and go live on a mountaintop, fellowshiping with the Lord. The Bible is very specific about our responsibilities as believers. Our roles as spouse, parent, employer, employee, etc., are all clearly articulated throughout Scripture. However, I would suggest that you and I are generally much better at any or all of those things than we are at our relationship with God.

> **This is not an uncommon occurrence for me: I am spending time in personal devotions, and after only a few brief moments, I begin to think about all the "important" things I could be doing.**

It's so easy to get caught up in the doing and miss what God is really interested in: relationship. Oswald Chambers said it like this, "The greatest competitor of devotion to Jesus is service for Him."

From the time I came into a saving relationship with Jesus Christ when I was in high school, I knew that the Lord's calling for my life was in ministry as a vocation. Over the next twelve years I worked various non-ministry jobs (and attended seminary), waiting for the fulfillment of that which God had placed in my heart.

All during this time I had an idea in the back of my mind that once I was in vocational ministry on a full-time basis everything would be different. I thought that once the goal of being full-time in ministry was attained there would then be more time for prayer, Bible study, seeking the Lord, etc.

The truth is that even today, in the midst of the very thing that the Lord has called me to do, it is still my choice. So often I find myself drawn to this project and that crisis—all the various things vying for my attention each and every day—and missing the One that is really important.

This is not an uncommon occurrence for me: I am spending time in personal devotions—prayer, Bible reading/study, worship—and after only a few brief moments, I begin to think about all the "important" things I could be doing. I remember that there is so much work to be done. I recall all of the pressing needs that are crying out to be completed, and I think that perhaps I should be doing something "more productive." All too frequently I give in to the temptation to go and work instead of simply doing what is really important: cultivating my relationship with the Lord.

"But," you may respond, "there are so many things that I *need* to do." It's true. It's the same in my life. The truth is that we are fairly proficient at most of those things. In our relationship with God we are too often much less skilled.

It is all too common to get caught up in *doing* all kinds of seemingly important things and forget that what God really wants is *relationship*.

Each of us can easily fall into this trap. It is all too common to get caught up in *doing* all kinds of seemingly important things and forget that what God really wants is *relationship*.

The first section of Revelation 2 is God's message to the church in Ephesus. He says this: "I know your deeds, your hard work and your perseverance. I know that you cannot tolerate wicked men, that you have tested those who claim to be apostles but are not, and have found them false. You have persevered and have endured hardships for My name, and have not grown weary" (Revelation 2:2-3). As I read these words, I would have considered it a great honor to be a part of such a group of people. The Lord is commending them for such praiseworthy items as "perseverance," "endured hardships," "not grown weary," and more. These are good things that they have been doing. I would love to hear my Savior say those words to me!

Unfortunately, the very next phrase is far less positive. "Yet I hold this against you: You have forsaken your first love" (Revelation 2:4). What an indictment! They were doing lots of good things, but they had missed the One that was really important. They had forgotten what was *really* important: relationship with God.

The Apostle Paul seemed to understand the need for this relationship: "What is more, I consider everything a loss compared to the surpassing greatness of knowing Christ Jesus my Lord, for whose sake I have lost all things. I consider them rubbish, that I may gain Christ" (Philippians 3:8).

What a statement! This is Paul, the apostle. Paul, a brilliant man. Well-educated. Righteous. The Pharisee's Pharisee. Outgoing. Friendly. Well-traveled. Articulate. But he says that none of these things make any difference compared to knowing Christ.

Please notice in Paul's statement that he did not say, "knowing *about* Christ Jesus..." The Greek word very clearly indicates not just head knowledge but relationship.

When my oldest son, David, graduated from sixth grade in a small Christian school, the parents of the class were invited to a luncheon and brief ceremony. The teacher asked each of the parents to share a section of Scripture with their child during the celebration. When my turn came, I shared Philippians 3:8. I explained to David that he reminded me a lot of Paul. "You're articulate and well-educated. You've gotten straight A's in everything this year. You're friendly. You're persuasive in speech. However, the reality is that without your relationship with the Lord, none of these things are of any value at all." The same is true for each one of us.

It is time for us all to "consider everything a loss compared to the surpassing greatness of knowing Christ Jesus my Lord." If the Holy Spirit is speaking anything universally to the church in North America, it is this: know God. Nothing is more important for us in this hour. Make your relationship with God the main priority of your life.

Personal application:

1. Is there a specific area of your service to God where you have been more focused on doing the things involved for that area than in knowing Him and His heart? If so, what steps do you need to take to rectify the situation?

2. Who are you more like, Mary or Martha? Does this need to change? If so, in what way?

3. Write a prayer that sums up your fresh commitment to make knowing God a priority in your life. Ask God to show you how and enable you do this.

Part 2

The Foundation for Our Relationship With God

Chapter 6

God's Grace:
Our Foundation

$\mathcal{S}$ome time ago I attended a Christian conference at which an elderly man, a respected teacher in the Body of Christ, was sharing. At one point someone asked him, "What is the most significant thing that has helped you in your walk as a Christian?" The man took almost no time to ponder what I thought would be a very soul-searching question. He simply responded that the most important thing he had learned to do over the years was to preach the gospel to himself every day. "Nothing else," he said, "has the power to cause change in our lives like the gospel." He had tried nearly everything else, but only the ongoing application of God's love and mercy had any lasting value.

If you have ever read the writings of the Apostle Paul (especially the letter to the church at Rome), you will agree that this statement is true. Again and again Paul comes back to the principle of grace. He repeatedly emphasizes it to make a point: The message of God's love is not just another teaching to be added in with many others. It is the undergirding message of all the rest.

> **This message of God's love is not just another teaching to be added in with many others. It is the undergirding message of all the rest.**

The truth is that God's love is much too large for us to comprehend. It is like the average citizen in our country trying to grasp the size of the national debt. Umpteen trillion dollars are way too gigantic for us to fathom. We have nothing to which we can compare such a concept. It's the same with God's love. We know of no other love that is so all-encompassing. The love of God is the single most powerful force there is, and yet it has been freely given to you and to me. Thank God for His indescribable gift of love!

Many years ago when I was in seminary, one of the professors in a particular class asked how many had had their lives radically changed when they began to realize the fullness of the love of God. Almost everyone in the class raised his hand. Truly opening your heart to God's love is life-changing.

In the book of Romans, Paul says: "I am not ashamed of the gospel, because it is the power of God for the salvation of everyone who believes..." (Romans 1:16). In order to understand this overall concept, we must first understand these words. Most Christians know that gospel means "good news," but good news about what?

The gospel can be summarized in the words of John 3:16: "For God so loved the world that He gave His one and only Son, that whoever believes in Him shall not perish but have eternal life." Why did God give His Son? Because of His love. Through that love the

Lord provided a way for us to have relationship with Him again. Through the Son, fellowship with God has been restored. All because of His great love.

His unfailing love is the heart of the entire gospel message. God's mercy, grace, and compassion toward us is His main motivation in dealing with us. We absolutely must understand this foundation in order to truly be in right relationship with Him.

"For I am not ashamed of the gospel, *for it is the power of God* for salvation to every one who believes..." It is interesting to note that Paul did not say that the gospel contains the facts *about* the power of God. Although he would have been correct in making such a statement, that was not his intent. Instead he stated very clearly: "The gospel *is* the power of God..." If you could make a mathematical equation out of that sentence, it might look like this: gospel=power of God. There is power in simply believing the gospel, the good news that God loves us so much that He sent Jesus to die in our place so that we might have forgiveness of sins.

Paul continues his statement with these words "...for salvation..." At this point many Christians see this verse as applying only to their initial conversion—when they were born-again. The truth of the matter is that the Greek word for "salvation" in this verse means far more than just being saved from hell. It encompasses the entire redemption (from sin, from the curse of the law, for the ongoing sanctification process, etc.) that Jesus purchased for us on the cross.

Understand then that the gospel *is* the *power* of God not just for the first step into the kingdom of God but for the ongoing keeping of those who have been brought into a saving relationship. It includes the initial conversion as well as the ongoing "cleaning up of our act." As believers, we need that power each and every day.

One commentator put it this way:

> All the effects of the gospel on the human heart are, in the Scriptures, traced to the power of God...There are no moral means which have ever been used that have such power as the gospel; none through which God has done so much in changing the character and affecting the destiny of man.[1]

Two major theological concepts—justification and sanctification—are seldom directly mentioned in this book, but the ideas are prevalent throughout the book. Therefore, a brief understanding of these concepts is in order here.

Justification means that we have already been made righteous by Jesus' sacrifice on the cross. There is nothing we can do to earn God's love and approval. It is only by accepting the finished work of Calvary that we are justified.

Sanctification, on the other hand, is the ongoing process of our lives being changed to be more like Jesus. It could be summed up in a statement I heard once: "God loves you just like you are, but He loves you too much to leave you that way."

Justification is instantaneous. Sanctification goes on for a life-time. Both, however, are a work of God's grace.

Have you found that beating on yourself (mentally, verbally, or physically) when you blow it (sin literally means "to miss the mark") yields no extra power to change? If we simply repent, however, and allow the mercies of the Lord to flood our being, we will find ourselves beginning to walk in His power, rather than in our own inconsistent strength.

Do you recall the time Jesus was being tempted by satan in the wilderness? When we look at that section of Scripture, we often see the first temptation as satan suggesting Jesus turn stones into bread. Although this was a wise temptation—Jesus had been fasting for forty days and was undoubtedly hungry—it was not the first.

The first temptation is found in satan's first seven words: "If you are the Son of God..." (Matthew 4:3). He was questioning Jesus' relationship with the Father. And he does the same thing to you and me. "*You*, a child of God?! After what you did today?! Not a chance!" Or, "You're not *really* a Christian! Just take a look at your life!" How many times have you heard those words or something similar questioning your relationship with your heavenly Father? It is exactly the same tactic satan used on Jesus.

The father of lies continues to use the same strategy on us for one simple reason: he knows that if he can get us to question our relationship with God, then he has effectively unplugged us from the only power source that will ever really make a difference in our lives. We must recognize that God's love is real and it is for us. And it is through that love that God will make changes in our lives.

My pastor has a cross-stitch wall-hanging in a very prominent spot in his office. It says this:

To run and work the law demands,
   but gives me neither feet nor hands.
Better news the gospel brings:
   it bids me fly and gives me wings.

The simple gospel message of God's amazing love for us contains a power that we will find in no other source.

A number of years ago while I was reading Ephesians, I realized anew the power of God's love and mercy within my life. Paul prays "...that you, being rooted and established in love, may have power, together with all the saints, to grasp how wide and long and high and deep is the love of Christ, and to know this love that surpasses knowledge—*that you may be filled to the measure of all the fullness of God*" (Ephesians 3:17-19, author's emphasis). What a statement! Paul is saying that when we begin to understand and walk in God's love, we will be filled up with God!

> **Paul is saying that when we begin to understand and walk in God's love, we will be filled up with God!**

Do you suppose it would make a difference in your life if you were "filled to the measure of all the fullness of God"? Of course it would. How, then, is that going to happen? By working for Him more diligently? Nope. According to this passage even praying more or studying the Bible more are not the things that will cause us to be filled up to the fullness of God, although these will ultimately be by-products of knowing His love. We will be filled up to the fullness of God only when we comprehend and believe that God loves us as much as He does. We must believe the gospel.

If we could begin to grasp this seemingly simple concept, I am completely convinced that we would see major changes within our lives and ministries.

God loves you. Period. And the only thing that will ultimately make a difference in you is that love—the gospel, the power of God. Nothing else will bring lasting change.

Personal application:

1. How would you describe God to someone who had never heard about Him before?

2. What difference has God's grace made in your life? You may recall a specific time when God was gracious to you or you may reflect on His graciousness over your whole life.

3. Do you see the gospel as the source of actual power in your life that enables change in you?

$\mathcal{S}$inners, Every One

$\mathcal{S}$in is an enemy of grace because it separates us from God. How we deal with our sin either reunites us with our loving Lord or drives us further from Him.

God's grace. Forgiveness of sins. This is the very core of what our faith is all about: sin and redemption. Too often people in the church try other cures for the problems in our society. We see political problems,

How we deal with our sin either reunites us with our loving Lord or drives us further from Him.

so we endeavor to pass wholesome legislation and elect godly politicians. We perceive economic woes, so we make efforts to stimulate the economy and help the poor. We see a complete breakdown of morality, so we try to get people to act in a more acceptable manner.

All of these can be good, even godly actions on our part, but each of these scenarios is only dealing with a symptom of the real problem. The base issue is sin. These other things are only the results of sin.

If man's true problem were his political woes, God would have sent a great statesman. If it were economic troubles, we would have been given an economist. Had the real problem been simply moral in nature, a fine teacher of morality would have been sufficient. Although Jesus was, in some measure, all of these, He was much more. God knew that man's most basic problem was sin, so He sent a Savior.

A rather prevalent teaching today says that once we become Christians we are no longer sinners. (Not that we no longer sin but that we are no longer sin*ners*.) Although I would dearly love to believe this, I cannot because it is contrary to Scripture.

In his first letter to Timothy, the Apostle Paul said this: "Christ Jesus came into the world to save sinners—of whom I am the worst. But for that very reason I was shown mercy so that in me, the worst of sinners, Christ Jesus might display His unlimited patience" (1 Timothy 1:15-16).

When Paul wrote this letter to Timothy, he had been a Christian for many years. At the time of the writing, he was not an unbeliever nor even a recent convert. He was a mature believer and an apostle. Yet in spite of all of this he says: "Christ Jesus came into the world to save sinners—of whom I *am* the worst." He doesn't say, "I *was* the worst sinner." He says, "I *am*..." The Greek verb form here is very plain. Paul is clearly identifying himself as a sinner when he wrote this.

Please realize that I am aware that we should not simply stop with that understanding. The Bible says that we have been made new creatures in Christ and that we have been made the righteousness of God in Christ (2 Corinthians 5:17, 21). It appears that those truths are more where our focus should be: dwelling on what God has done for us. However, when we dwell only there, it is easy to cross a line into thinking that we have become immune to sin.

A pastor friend once told me about a woman in his church who shared with him that God had placed a shield around her against temptation. She was certain that she would never be tempted by sin again. The pastor patiently listened and then explained that if anyone had told her that, it was more likely the enemy of our souls. She refused to listen to his counsel and left. Several months later the woman divorced her husband because he was "not spiritual enough." When we think we are impervious to sin, we are being set up for trouble.

Perhaps the great reformer, Martin Luther, described our situation best. He said that as Christians we are both saint and sinner at the same time. We are forgiven and stand holy in the sight of God. Yet at the same time we are in desperate need of the Lord's grace and mercy and forgiveness all the time.

Some people say, "I am not schizophrenic. I am not part sinner and part saint. I am the righteousness of God in Christ." That sounds pious enough, but by that "logic," then Paul, the apostle, was inspired by the Holy Spirit to be schizophrenic. Confessing the truth of God's Word can be a very good thing for us. However, we must be careful to confess the whole truth and not just the parts we like best.

C.S. Lewis had a unique way of looking at this concept. In his book *Perelandra*, the second book in his fantasy space trilogy, two angels are discussing man.

"Look on him, beloved, and love him," said the first. "He is indeed but breathing dust and a careless touch would unmake him. And in his best thoughts are such things mingled as, if we thought them, our lights would perish. But he is in the body of [Christ] and his sins are forgiven."[1]

Even as believers, we are sinners in need of God's grace every moment of every day.

In all of this, please realize that I am not attempting to diminish the awfulness of our sin. Sin is heinous. Nothing is more loathsome in the sight of God. Sin is the thing that sent Jesus to the cross. Any sin is a terrible, despicable act.

However, the grace of God is always greater than sin. The unfailing love of the Lord will always be more powerful. In reality, this is the power over sin: the gospel.

Let me also be clear that I am not suggesting that because of grace we have a license to sin. Paul addresses this issue very plainly (and very strongly) in the sixth chapter of Romans. In answer to the questions, "Shall we sin?" (v. 15) and "Shall we go on sinning?" (v. 1) he gives the same answer: "By no means!" The term used in these exclamatory remarks is the strongest possible negative Greek word. Paul is saying, "Absolutely, positively not!" He does, however, consistently give us the cure for sin throughout the book of Romans: it is God's unmerited favor through Jesus' atoning work on the cross. Paul repeatedly points us to God's great grace as the answer to the sin problem.

> **Reconciling sinners to be in right relationship with the Father is the whole purpose of the cross. When we attempt to justify our sin...we have completely missed the power of reconciliation.**

This is not, as some have suggested, "cheap grace." In his book *The Grace Awakening*, Chuck Swindoll quotes Dietrich Bonhoeffer: "Cheap grace justifies the sin rather than the sinner. True grace, on the other hand, justifies the sinner, not the sin."[2]

Reconciling sinners to be in right relationship with the Father is the whole purpose of the cross. When we attempt to justify our sin ("It wasn't really that important. It was just a little sin."), we have completely missed the power of reconciliation.

My pastor recently made a statement that struck me. He said, "The forgiveness of sins has a catch: it's only for the guilty." There is lack of understanding in the North American church that we are guilty. We are much more apt to blame-shift or use self-justification. However, it is only when we honestly confess our sins with a heart attitude of true repentance that there can be true forgiveness.

Jesus told a story that illustrates this point:

> Two men went up to the temple to pray, one a Pharisee and the other a tax collector. The Pharisee stood up and prayed about himself: "God, I thank you that I am not like other men—robbers,

evildoers, adulterers—or even like this tax collector..." But the tax collector stood at a distance. He would not even look up to heaven, but beat his breast and said, "God, have mercy on me, a sinner." I tell you that this man, rather than the other, went home justified before God" (Luke 18:10-14).

If the "self-esteem gospel" that is so prevalent today were actually true, then the Pharisee would have been okay and not the tax collector. In order for forgiveness to occur, we must recognize the wretchedness of our situation. We must realize how desperately we need God's cleansing forgiveness.

The real purpose of the law (all of the do's and don't's of the Bible) is to push us toward the Lord. "So the law was put in charge to lead us to Christ that we might be justified by faith" (Galatians 3:24). It demonstrates how much we need God. Romans 3:20 says basically the same thing: "Therefore no one will be declared righteous in His (God's) sight by observing the law; rather, through the law we become conscious of sin." The job of the law is to show us that we are indeed sinners who desperately need God.

It is certainly not difficult to find laws (rules, commandments) from the Bible that we break. For example, "You shall not covet your neighbor's house...or anything that belongs to your neighbor" (Exodus 20:17). Have you ever wished you could have something that someone else owns? Or "Be completely humble and gentle..." (Ephesians 4:2). Are you always *completely* humble and gentle? When we break the laws of God, we have sinned.

Personally, I welcome the conviction of God in my life. You see, it is not conviction just about a bad attitude. Or about an unhealthy fear. Or lewd thoughts. Or a grudge. It may be any or all of these (or a myriad of other things), but first and foremost it is conviction of sin. And I know how to handle sin. Repent and accept God's unmerited grace in the form of Jesus' substitutionary death on the cross.

There is an involuntary reaction that causes us to pull back when we touch something hot. Pain in this instance is good. That's what guilt does for us. Without guilt we do not need grace. The day we lose our consciousness of sin is the day we no longer need Christ.

"You say, 'I am rich; I have acquired wealth and do not need a thing.' But you do not realize that you are wretched, pitiful, poor, blind and naked" (Revelation 3:17). These words were not written to unbelievers but to the believers at Laodicea. Jesus had just declared that they were not "cold" but "lukewarm." The problem was not that they were not saved but that they thought they were okay. They were self-righteous. They no longer needed God. In the midst of their self-assuredness, God calls them "wretched, pitiful, poor, blind and naked."

Prior to coming into the kingdom of God, how much of the law were we guilty of? Years later, if we have reached the point where there are fewer areas of sin in us, are we any less in need of forgiveness? No! "For whoever keeps the whole law and yet stumbles at just one point is guilty of breaking all of it" (James 2:10). We must recognize our guilt and cry out to God for forgiveness.

Of course there is another dimension to sin-consciousness that should be addressed. Often, when we begin to have an honest, godly consciousness of sin, the enemy of our souls tries to help it along. Feelings of hopelessness and total rejection are the outcome. Satan wants us to be aware of our sin to condemn us. God wants us to be aware of our sins in order for us to be forgiven.

In discussing sin and God's gracious forgiveness, we must additionally note that there very well may still be ongoing consequences to sin. The temporal results of our wrongdoings may not be altered by our repenting. If a man honestly repents to the Lord after robbing a grocery store, he quite probably will still be sent to prison. The earthly consequences of our actions are still evident most of the time. Yet even in the midst of those consequences, God still loves the sinner intensely.

The bottom line is this: there is sin in your life. "...everything that does not come from faith is sin" (Romans 14:23). Most of us probably do something "that does not come from faith" before we even brush our teeth in the morning. Recognizing and admitting that fact points us in the right direction. When I realize that I am a sinner and that there is nothing inherently good in me, then I am ready to admit that I am completely dependent on God.

Personal application:

1. It's easy to have the attitude of, "I'm a pretty good person." The truth is, we're not. Acknowledging the fact that you are indeed a sinner in need of His grace will go a long way toward strengthening your relationship with the Lord. Take a few minutes right now and talk candidly with God about your life.

2. Grace is real, but in order to receive it, we must first confess and repent of our sin. Is there an area of your life that you would rather not discuss, even with God? Guess what. He already knows about it. Be honest with the Lord, repent, and receive His forgiveness.

3. Are you at the point in your walk with God that you think you have fewer areas of sins? So few that you have little need for a Savior, since you're pretty good on your own? This is a dangerous place to be. Read James 2:10, "For whoever keeps the whole law and yet stumbles at just one point is guilty of breaking all of it," again and ask God to show you in a fresh, new way how much you need Him and His grace.

ur Heart Attitude

What God is really interested in more than anything is our heart. One of my favorite scriptural illustrations of this is found in 2 Chronicles 30. Hezekiah was the king of Judah. The nation was about to celebrate the Passover celebration for the first time in many years. The law clearly stated that the people must purify themselves in order to eat the Passover.

Although most of the people who came from Ephraim, Mannasseh, Issachar and Zebulun had not purified themselves, they ate the Passover, contrary to what was written. But Hezekiah prayed for them, saying, "May the LORD, Who is good, pardon everyone who sets his heart on seeking God—the LORD, the God of his fathers—even if he is not clean according to the rules of the sanctuary." And the LORD heard Hezekiah and healed the people (2 Chronicles 30:18-20).

Amazing. The actions of the people were completely wrong. Yet their hearts were right, and God chose to forgive.

Most assuredly the Lord wants our actions to reflect our love for Him, but the heart motivation is the key. "Man looks at the outward appearance, but the LORD looks at the heart" (1 Samuel 16:7b). The Old Testament prophets consistently denounced the Israelites' worship, not because they were doing the wrong things, but because their hearts were not in it. God always looks first at the heart. He knows that this side of heaven we are not going to be perfect and deals with us accordingly. "For He knows how we are formed, He remembers that we are dust" (Psalm 103:14). In spite of our actions, He looks at our hearts and sees that we desire to do the right thing.

There are some people who do not care when they sin. It makes absolutely no difference to them at all. They reach a point where their hearts are cold and calloused. They have no honest sorrow for their sins. There is no repentance, no desire to change. At that point they have made the choice to "deliberately keep on sinning..." and "trampled the Son of God under foot..." and "insulted the Spirit of grace" (Hebrews 10:26-29).

My experience has been that those people are rare in the Church. Most people loathe their sins. Their attitude is like Paul's in Romans 7. "I hate what I am doing!" As long as the heart is still longing for God, as long as the Holy Spirit is still bringing conviction, there will always be forgiveness.

I recently heard a Christian radio talk show. During the show, listeners were given the opportunity to call in and ask questions. At one point a young lady called and asked a couple of seemingly mundane questions. The host realized that the woman was skirting the issue for which she really called and directly asked her what her real question was. The caller began to cry. Through sobs and strained voice she confided that some Christian friends had told her that she had committed the unpardonable sin, blaspheming the Holy Spirit (see Mark 3:29) and that she could no longer be saved. She wanted to know what to do.

The talk-show host handled it perfectly. I didn't write down his exact words, but in essence he said this: "You did not commit the unpardonable sin. Please hear what I am saying to you. I am not saying, 'I don't think you did' or 'You probably did not.' I am telling you without any wavering or doubting that

> **In reality, consistently running to the Lord is more important than having your life all straightened out.**

you *did not* commit the unpardonable sin. I can say that, even without knowing the details of what you've done, because I can hear your repentance. If you had committed the unforgivable sin, your heart would be completely hard. There would be no regret. You would be cold and hard and calloused. But you're not. You are very obviously sincerely sorry for whatever it is that you have done. With that kind of heart attitude, God will always take you back and offer forgiveness."

He is exactly right. The important point to the Lord is our heart attitude. If we are not repentant, if we really don't care about our sins, then we are truly lost. However, if there is a sincere desire for change, a sincere repentance in our hearts, God always offers forgiveness. In reality, consistently running to the Lord is more important than having your life all straightened out.

The real issue in all of this is how we handle our sin. Almost always we act like Adam. When he and Eve heard God coming to the garden after they had eaten from the forbidden tree, they tried to hide from Him. Does it make any sense to you (it certainly doesn't to me) that Adam thought he could hide from God? Unfortunately, we frequently try to do the same type of thing.

Let's be really candid for a moment. When you do whatever it is that distances you from the Lord, what do you do next? You turn on the television. Or read the newspaper. Or go to the refrigerator. Right? Or perhaps for you it is some other mindless take-me-away-from-reality endeavor. Whatever it may be, the idea is to do anything at all except looking face-to-face into the eyes of a holy God because that is too revealing and we just can't bear it. We know we have fallen short, and we think that putting distance between ourselves and the Lord is the best way to handle it.

Isn't that just like our sinful nature? We attempt to deal with the problem in a way that is totally opposite from God's plan. Instead, He would have us turn to Him in repentance and find grace and forgiveness from our loving heavenly Father. We must understand that from God's perspective the price has already been paid. His attitude toward us in those situations is, "Don't run away from Me; run to Me."

Again, what God is interested in is our hearts. Some people who profess to be Christians engage in practices that the Bible clearly refers to as sin. These people see nothing wrong with their actions. Some even flaunt them. However, because there is no heart repentance, there can never be forgiveness.

> ...there are two groups of people in the world: there are the sinners who admit they are sinners and the sinners who refuse to admit their sin.

You and I also sin every day. In all honesty, from God's perspective there is no difference in the awfulness of our sin and the sin of the people I just mentioned. The difference is that you and I, just like the Apostle Paul, are devastated by our sin. We are repentant, and because we are repentant, there will always be forgiveness.

For centuries people have had the idea that there are two groups of people in the world: the "good folks" and the "sinners." The truth is that there are two groups of people, but from a scriptural perspective I would have to label the categories a bit differently. There are the sinners who admit they are sinners and the sinners who refuse to admit their sin.

In reality, the essential nature of sin is not the deeds but the heart. Scripture tells us that every inclination of man's heart is evil from childhood (Genesis 8:21). Jesus told us that if we hate our brother it is the same as murder. God looks first at the heart. Even if we are completely pure from an outward perspective, our hearts still need to be cleansed and changed. And the only way that will happen is by consistently turning to the One who loves us intensely.

When a child does wrong, what is it that a parent hopes will result from disciplining the child? If you could, without spanking, without raising your voice, achieve a desired result in the child, what would that result be? Obviously, we need to rule out perfect sinlessness because that will not happen this side of heaven. What then would be the desired result? I pondered that question one day and finally arrived at the obvious answer: that the remorse over the sin would be an even stronger discipline than what I could verbally or physically administer. That the agony over doing wrong would be far more painful than any spanking or harsh words. In other words, my goal is that there would be genuine, heart-felt repentance. That's exactly what God is looking for from His children.

Even if our actions look good, we may very well have sin "hidden" in our hearts. On the other hand, when our hearts are turned to God to repent, He is willing and able to forgive even the sin in our hearts that separates us from Him.

Personal application:

1. How is your heart attitude? Is there anything you know is sin but you are trying to hide from God and cover it up?

2. Is there an area in your life where your actions are "right," but you know your heart attitude is all wrong? For example, relating to others at your church or even serving at church.

3. Are you willing to pray with the psalmist: "Create in me a pure heart, O God, and renew a steadfast spirit within me"? (Psalm 51:10). Do that right now. Spend some time opening your heart to the Lord.

Chapter 9

Here I Am Again, Lord

How could God possibly love me? I have failed Him over and over again. Even though I know better, I still blow it. He could not possibly still care about me, could He?"

I cannot begin to tell you the number of times I have heard these thoughts from people all across the nation. It has probably been on the lips of, or, at the very least, on the mind of practically everyone who has ever been a part of the kingdom of God. I know I have felt like this more times than I care to remember. Every one of us at some point in life has felt as though we have failed the Lord by our actions or words. Most of the time the problem is not that we are unaware of our sin but that we are all too aware of our consistent failings.

Of all the problems that weigh down believers today, the most prevalent is a failure to comprehend or fully believe the power of the gospel of Jesus. As I travel and talk with Christians, the thing they seem to despise the most is their own consistent inadequacies and failures before the Lord.

> **As I travel and talk with Christians, the thing they seem to despise the most is their own consistent inadequacies and failures before the Lord.**

All of us have areas of weakness with which we struggle. Obviously these areas are different for different people. Some struggle with greed or impatience. Others with lust or hatred or overeating. Still others battle evil thoughts or a desire for power. The list could go on. However, those weaknesses all have one thing in common: they are the things we do over and over again, even when we know better.

Often, the longer we walk with the Lord, the more difficult it is to accept His love. We often feel the way Paul must have felt when he wrote Romans 7: "For what I do is not the good I want to do; no, the evil I do not want to do—this I keep on doing" (Romans 7:19). And in the midst of that struggle we cannot fathom how God could possibly love us. Further along in the same chapter Paul sinks even further. "What a wretched man I am! Who will rescue me from this body of death?" (Romans 7:24). Have you ever struggled with that type of feeling? With this attitude, we begin to try in our own strength to do better, to act more like we think a Christian should act.

Many years ago I was overwhelmed by a struggle with a particular area of sin in my own life. After having fallen into the trap of this sin once again, I was devastated by what I had done. How could I, having walked with the Lord for nearly three years, still be doing the same things I had renounced many times over? I was convinced that I had crossed the line into sin one too many times and now God was through with me. He could never possibly love me again. With all of these condemning thoughts stirring in my mind I spent the next couple of hours crying and wallowing in self-pity.

I had been outdoors during this time, and as I walked back inside my home, the telephone rang. It was my then-girlfriend, now-wife, and by the tone of my voice, she knew something was wrong. I explained the situation. I told her I was devastated by the fact that I had been a Christian for nearly three years, but I was often doing some of the same sinful acts I had done before giving my heart and life to the Lord. She listened patiently, and when I had finished, she made a statement that still impacts my life to this day: "It's true. But God still loves you. He still cares."

As soon as she said it, something inside me shattered, and I realized the truth of those words. All of a sudden my entire perspective changed. I was still devastated by my sinful acts, but I realized anew God's love and grace. My two hours of crying did nothing. Those four seconds' worth of words about God's love changed me completely. Why? Because it was the gospel, the power of God.

It is knowing God's love that changes us, yet so often we find ourselves drifting from that knowledge again and again. Of course we do not shift away from the foundation of the Lord's great love on purpose. It is usually more of an unconscious action on our part. The temptation is to try harder. However, when we give in to that temptation, we have put ourselves back under the law and are no longer walking in the gospel.

> **Trying harder will not blot out sin. Only Jesus can do that.**

Trying harder will not blot out sin. Only Jesus can do that.

There is exactly one cure for man's basic problem: the blood that Jesus shed at Calvary. It is the only acceptable means of dealing with sin. But there is something innately opposed to God's free gift within the hearts and minds of mankind. Grace is just not logical.

Let's look at this from a different angle. When someone with a despicable, carnal, anti-God background becomes born-again, our normal reaction is, "It took a miracle." But let's be really candid for a moment. Do you honestly think it was less of a miracle for God to save a respectable sinner like you? Furthermore, do you think it takes any less of a miracle to keep you in His kingdom day by day?

Of course not. It is only His great love and new-every-morning mercies (Lamentations 3:23) that keep us going.

"But God demonstrates His own love for us in this: *While we were still sinners*, Christ died for us" (Romans 5:8, author's emphasis). At some point in your life, did the Lord draw you into His kingdom? Did He forgive you when you were born-again? Do you think that maybe, just maybe, He knew beforehand the failures you would commit after you became a Christian? Of course He did.

In light of this, was He just toying with you then, or is His forgiveness far-reaching enough to have effect even now? Obviously, even though He was fully aware of how you would fail, the Lord still called you into His kingdom. His grace is sufficient.

God's love is real. He does not love you any more after you become a Christian than He did prior to your conversion. He also does not love you any less when you, as a Christian, sin. (Of course He does not like or condone your sin, but His love remains the same.) "I have loved you with an *everlasting love*; I have drawn you with lovingkindness" (Jeremiah 31:3, author's emphasis).

Unquestionably, we have failed the Lord many times and will continue to do so. For this reason, God has made a way for us to find forgiveness and acceptance through Jesus' atoning work on Calvary. When we confess our sins with a heart to turn from them, the blood of Jesus truly does wash away our sins (1 John 1:9).

Personal application:

1. In what area(s) do you struggle again and again with a certain sin? Have you repented of this sin and accepted Jesus' substitutionary death on the cross as the payment for your sin? If yes, do you believe that you are forgiven and that God still loves you?

2. How long have you been a Christian? Do you ever struggle with thoughts about how, after that length of time, you should really try to be a better Christian? How should you handle those kind of thoughts?

3. What does it mean to you to know that God still loves you, even when you fail?

Chapter 10

No Waiting Necessary

Do you remember the story of the prodigal son? The son had taken everything that he owned and deliberately squandered it in sin. He became a desperate and broken man and decided to return home, admit his sin, and live as a servant.

The prodigal quite probably came to a point where he felt like David did when he wrote Psalm 32:

"Blessed is he whose transgressions are forgiven, whose sins are covered. Blessed is the man whose sin the LORD does not count against him and in whose spirit is no deceit. *When I kept silent, my bones wasted away through my groaning all day long. For day and night Your hand was heavy upon me; my strength was sapped as in the heat of summer*" (Psalm 32:1-4, author's emphasis).

The Holy Spirit brought conviction to David's heart because of his sin and would not let him rest until it was dealt with. However, that is not the end of the story. "Then I acknowledged my sin to You and did not cover up my iniquity. I said, 'I will confess my transgressions to the LORD'—*and You forgave the guilt of my sin*" (Psalm 32:5, author's emphasis). There appears to be no time lag between the confession of the sin and the forgiveness. David repented and God forgave.

> **One major reason we have difficulty accepting God's forgiveness immediately is because of our own human experiences.**

That sounds a lot like the conclusion to the prodigal saga. As the son came home to repent, the father saw him coming from a long way off and ran to him. Before the young man could even finish speaking, the father accepted him back, not as a servant, but as his son. In telling this parable, Jesus was portraying an image of our loving heavenly Father who stands waiting for us to come with repentant hearts and be accepted by Him. If we will turn to Him, asking for forgiveness, He reaches out to us.

The Apostle John clearly told us: "If we confess our sins, He is faithful and just and will forgive us our sins and purify us from all unrighteousness" (1 John 1:9). Those words were written to believers. Our job is to confess. God's job is to forgive and purify.

One major reason we have difficulty accepting God's forgiveness immediately is because of our own human experiences. Usually when someone has wronged us we have trouble truly offering immediate forgiveness. Often, even if we say the right words (i.e., "I forgive you."), we still want them to maintain an ongoing repentant attitude for a certain length of time. It makes us feel better.

I remember the day one of my children broke something that was very valuable. We took care of the entire incident in a proper manner...except for my heart. I verbalized my forgiveness, but inside, because of the sentimental value of the broken object, I still felt distant from my child. Unfortunately, I portrayed the distant feeling by my actions. It was obvious to both of us that I had not *really* forgiven.

Situations like this shape and mold our perceptions of what God is like. It is difficult for us to go beyond our human experiences. We are certain that God, too, must feel distant from us until a certain amount of time has passed. Perhaps tomorrow we can again be intimate with God, but certainly not today.

God is not like that. He does not hold grudges. His forgiveness is real and immediate.

When we insist on being removed from the Lord for a certain amount of time, we have placed ourselves back under the law. And there is no justification under the law (Galatians 2:21).

Paul understood God's forgiveness when he wrote Romans. Although he bared his heart in chapter seven ("For what I do is not the good I want to do; no, the evil I do not want to do—this I keep on doing... What a wretched man I am!") the entire scenario changes in chapter eight. What truth and reality Paul found when he opened his heart to the grace and mercy of God—the simple message that the Lord of all creation loves us. "For I am convinced that neither death nor life, neither angels nor demons, neither the present nor the future, nor any powers, neither height nor depth, nor anything else in all creation, will be able to separate us from the love of God that is in Christ Jesus our Lord" (Romans 8:38-39). Just one chapter later, Paul is a changed man. It is because he was now walking in God's grace and not just looking at all the ways that he does not follow God's laws.

More than "beating" ourselves mentally when we fall short, what we need is a fresh understanding of God's unmerited favor.

The message of the gospel has been referred to as an amazing double transfer. Everything that is vile and evil in us is transferred to Jesus, and everything that is good and right in Jesus is transferred to us. He takes our sin, and we stand credited with every righteous thought, word, and deed ever performed by the Lord Jesus while He was here on earth (Isaiah 53:6; Galatians 3:13; Philippians 3:9; Romans 5:18; 2 Corinthians 5:21).

When we reach out to God to make this amazing transfer, the transaction is immediate—no waiting necessary.

Personal application:

1. Are there ways that you related to your family and others when you were growing up that hinder you from really believing that God's forgiveness is real and immediate?

2. If yes, perhaps it would help for you to do a study of the word "forgive" as it is used in the Bible to know what God's forgiveness is really like. Using a concordance, look up the word "forgive" and see what the Bible has to say about this topic.

3. Are you still "punishing" yourself or staying away from intimacy with God because of something you did, even though you've repented already (maybe even more than once)?

Chapter 11

You Cannot Earn the Gift

Imagine a preschool-age girl bringing a gift to her daddy. She tells him it's a special gift just for him because she loves him so much. She's wrapped it herself. He can tell. The box has as much tape as it does wrapping paper. It takes a while for him to open it. All the while, his daughter grins at him. She squirms and giggles as he works to get it open. He can tell she's very proud of her gift and very excited to see his reaction to her treasure. As he forces open the last bit of tape and lifts the lid to the small box, his daughter presses closer to him unable to decide whether she should look at his face or the gift. She squeals with delight and begins to clap her hands and jump up and down as he lifts her precious gift from its box.

Her daddy works hard to keep smiling and seem happy. He's lifted out of the box a rag—a filthy, smelly rag. Yet it is obvious this is indeed a special gift when his daughter says, "Don't you love it, Daddy? I made it just for you! I worked hard. I love you so much, Daddy. I'll go make some more for you." Daddy is left to prepare to respond as she skips off to bring him more of her worthless, even offensive, "treasures."

The prophet Isaiah said: "...all our righteous acts are like filthy rags" (Isaiah 64:6). All of the good things we do in our own strength are like filthy rags to God. Somehow, I really don't think that the Lord cares all that much for our "treasures" of all our good deeds.

Unfortunately, we often act like the little girl, rushing to God to offer what we think is something really special. The truth is that all those good things we do, in and of themselves, are worthless in God's sight. He does not see them as treasures. From the Lord's perspective, by their own merit, they are filthy rags.

Most Christians, especially those who came into the kingdom of God later in life, point to the message of a loving, forgiving God as to what initially drew them into the kingdom. The concept that "God loves me just as I am," is a compelling force. Unfortunately, all too often, the longer we are a part of the kingdom of God, the further we drift from this original foundation.

It appears from Scripture that there were teachers who were endeavoring to "undo" the gospel message preached by Paul (see especially Paul's letter to the Galatians). These men wanted to convince the Gentile believers that they must obey all of the Old Testament rules in order to be saved. The truth is that straying from the pure gospel is the Church's most consistent heresy throughout the ages.

Author Max Lucado, in his book *No Wonder They Call Him Savior*, said it this way:

> It happened too fast. One minute Barabbas was in his cell on death row playing Tic-Tac-Toe on the dirt walls, and the next he was outside squinting his eyes at the bright sun.

"You're free to go."

Barabbas scratches his beard. "What?"

"You're free. They took the Nazarene instead of you."

Barabbas has often been compared to humanity, and rightly so. In many ways he stands for us: a prisoner who was freed because someone he had never seen took his place.

But I think Barabbas was probably smarter than we are in one respect.

As far as I know, he took his sudden freedom for what it was, an undeserved gift. Someone tossed him a life preserver and he grabbed it, no questions asked. You couldn't imagine him pulling some of our stunts. We take our free gift and try to earn it or diagnose it or pay for it instead of simply saying "thank you" and accepting it.

Ironic as it may appear, one of the hardest things to do is be saved by grace. There's something in us that reacts to God's free gift. We have some weird compulsion to create laws, systems, and regulations that will make us "worthy" of our gift.

Why do we do that? The only reason I can figure is pride. To accept grace means to accept its necessity, and most folks don't like to do that. To accept grace also means that one realizes his despair, and most people aren't too keen on doing that either.[1]

In some ways I think this statement may be even more true for us after we become a Christian. We still have trouble, perhaps even more trouble, accepting His grace after we have come into a relationship with the Lord. We have shifted from our original foundation.

In his letter to the church of Galatia, Paul addresses the concept of shifting off of our original foundation of God's grace. In very strong terms he says: "You foolish Galatians! Who has bewitched you?...I would like to learn just one thing from you: Did you receive the Spirit by observing the law, or by believing what you heard? Are you so foolish? After beginning with the Spirit, are you now trying to attain your goal by human effort?" (Galatians 3:1-3). Later in the same letter Paul states his case further: "You who are trying to be justified by law have been alienated from Christ; you have fallen away from grace" (Galatians 5:4).

The Galatian Christians were trying to do exactly the same thing we often try to do: having begun their walk with the Lord by His grace, they began to strive in their own strength to do better. They became focused on works and what they could do to earn God's love. It did not work then, and it will not work today.

> **The Galatian Christians were trying to do exactly the same thing we often try to do: having begun their walk with the Lord by His grace, they began to strive in their own strength to do better.**

Many people endeavor to attain a certain level of sinlessness in their lives with the idea that this will make them more acceptable to God. The letter to the church at Colosse offers thoughts on this attitude. Paul is discussing submitting to rules such as, "Do not handle! Do not taste! Do not touch!" (Colossians 2:21). He goes on to say: "Such regulations indeed have an appearance of wisdom...*but they lack any value in restraining sensual indulgence*" (Colossians 2:23, author's emphasis). Forcing yourself to do and not do certain things is not the ultimate answer.

Please understand that I am not suggesting there is no value in self-discipline. In fact, there can be a great deal of value in self-discipline. In this hour the Church needs far more self-discipline than we have often practiced in the past. However, the truth is that you can put on a veneer of spirituality, but that will not and cannot cause God to love you any more than He already does.

It is so easy to focus on doing good things because our actions are clearly a part, even a big part, of becoming Christ-like. James makes it clear that our faith without action is dead. Paul, in his letters, encourages believers to do so many things such as praying without ceasing, being devoted to our families, and loving each other. Jesus' parables implied that we should care for those in prison and in need. The Great Commission to go into all the earth with the gospel message is full of needed action. There is certainly no lack of commandments that require constant action or purposeful restraint on our part in order to act as a Christian "should." And yet, as important as all these good things are, they are not what makes us acceptable to God. They are not what the Lord looks at as the sign that we are His. He looks for the blood of His Son that makes us righteous and worthy.

Do you remember the story of the rich young ruler who came to Jesus? He asked Jesus what he must do to inherit eternal life, and Jesus told him to obey the commandments. The man inquired as to which commandments, apparently a reference to the thousands of commandments compiled by the religious leaders of Israel. In response, Jesus begins to list out a few of the ten commandments, in essence saying, "The commandments of God." The man replies that he has kept all of them since he was a boy. Jesus' next words went directly to the man's heart. "'One thing you lack,' He said. 'Go sell everything you have and give to the poor...'" (Mark 10:21). That segment of the story ends with the young man leaving, very sad, "because he had great wealth" (Mark 10:22).

> You and I, also, have only one hope. It is not our own goodness or our own strength. It is not length of time in His kingdom. It is simply His love toward us. Our only hope is God's grace.

Jesus' obvious intent was to show this man that not only had he not kept the commandments, but he hadn't even kept the very first one, "You shall have no other gods before Me" (Exodus 20:3). His money had become his god. Jesus was endeavoring to show him that in spite of how good he thought he was, he was not good enough.

After the young man left, Jesus addressed His disciples. He told them that it is easier for a camel to go through the eye of a needle than for a rich man to be saved. The reaction of the disciples to the scenario was typical. "The disciples were even more amazed, and said to each other, 'Who then can be saved?'" (Mark 10:26).

Jesus' answer is perfect. "With man this is impossible, but not with God; all things are possible with God" (Mark 10:27). He was clearly showing them that man's own strength and abilities will never be enough. In essence He told them there is only one source for what is necessary for salvation: God. They could forget their own goodness and righteousness. It would never be enough. They needed only to look to God.

You and I, also, have only one hope. It is not our own goodness or our own strength. It is not length of time in His kingdom. It is simply His love toward us. Our only hope is God's grace.

As believers we often attempt to substitute practically anything and everything else for the grace of God. We try harder, endeavoring to act more like we think Christians should act.

A recurring tendency in the Church over the centuries is to lapse back into self-justification. We think that because of certain actions in our lives God will find us more acceptable. People in nearly every expression of the Body of Christ can easily fall into this trap. Those involved in the prayer movement can begin to believe that because they pray more frequently God likes them better than other Christians. Those who are a part of the current trend in praise and worship can think that the Lord finds them more acceptable because they sing more fervently than some other believers. Even Christians who pursue social action (feeding the hungry, ministering to prisoners, etc.) can assume that they are better than those who do not engage in such activities.

It is important to note that all of these can be very godly, very spiritual pursuits. However, none of them makes us more acceptable to God. Only the blood of Jesus does that. The Lord's grace and mercy are the only means by which we can be accepted by Him. Not even our most spiritual quests can cause God to love us more than He does right now.

A while back I had one of those beyond-hectic weeks. Unfortunately, in the midst of the turmoil, I had not taken as much time for prayer, personal worship, and Bible study as I would normally. When I got up on Sunday morning, I immediately heard very sarcastic thoughts in my mind: "With the week you've had, who are you to go and minister to God's people?" Fortunately, I had walked with the Lord long enough and had a firm enough foundation that I knew the right answer. I responded, "No one. I am simply a sinner saved by grace." That is the only foundation I have for anything that I do. I am completely and utterly dependent upon His mercy and grace in my life for *everything*. God's unfailing love is my one and only foundation.

I am not suggesting that time spent with the Lord in prayer and worship or the study of His Word are unimportant. On the contrary, these things will help solidify the foundation. But they do not make us more acceptable to God. They may make us more effective in accomplishing His purposes, but it is only His great love and grace that allow us to stand before Him in the first place.

Sometimes I find that I struggle with the opposite scenario. On the weeks when I do spend lots of time in prayer and personal devotions, I can have the attitude of being self-sufficient. I can think, "Of course the Lord is pleased with me. I've done all the right things this week; I've been good." At times like this, just as much as in the previous case, I need to return to my foundation of the grace of God. Only His grace, not my righteousness, allows me to stand before Him in any capacity.

I can never do enough to earn God's love. The good news is... I don't have to. Christ already proved His love through His ultimate sacrifice on the cross. In Galatians 2:21, Paul sums it up this way: "I do not set aside the grace of God, for if righteousness could be gained through the law, Christ died for nothing!"

We can never be good enough. We can never follow all of God's laws. It is only by Christ's death and resurrection that we are reunited with God. We can never earn the free gift of our salvation. We can never earn God's love. He gave it to us long before we ever loved Him. No matter what we do, He cannot love us more than He already does.

Personal application:

1. Are there any good deeds you do with an eye toward earning God's approval? Give an example.

2. What practical impact will genuinely accepting God's grace, instead of doing good deeds to earn God's favor, have in your life?

3. Do you really get this point? You can never earn God's love and acceptance. Why do you think so many people get caught in the trap of doing things for God in order to be loved and accepted by Him?

Chapter 12

*I*t All Begins
and Ends With
God's Grace

*M*y youngest son, Stephen, has a quilt with glow-in-the-dark material as part of the pattern. I'm sure you've seen glow-in-the-dark items and you know how they work. You place the item under a light, then put it in a dark room and it glows...for a while. Eventually it stops glowing. In order to get it to glow again, you have to put it back under the light. Do you understand the application of what I'm saying for *your* life? We were not designed to walk out this life apart from relationship with God. Without Him we're empty.

During His earthly ministry, Jesus said it like this: "I am the true vine...remain in Me, and I will remain in you. No branch can bear fruit by itself; it must remain in the vine. Neither can you bear fruit unless you remain in Me" (John 15:1-4). It is our relationship with Him that makes us able to do anything. Jesus continues by saying, "I am the vine; you are the branches. If a man remains in Me and I in him, he will bear much fruit; *apart from Me you can do nothing*" (John 15:5, author's emphasis). In order to accomplish anything at all, we must get our strength, our abilities, from Him. Apart from our relationship with Him, there is absolutely nothing of any lasting value that you or I will ever accomplish.

In the middle section of 2 Corinthians 12:9, God tells the Apostle Paul, "My power is made perfect in weakness." A dear friend of mine, Daryl Roth, has a favorite saying about his relationship with the Lord that is based on this passage. Daryl says, "I supply the weakness and God supplies the strength."

He's right. It is God's power living and active within us that begins and ends His work in us. "...for it is God who works in you to will and to act according to his good purpose" (Philippians 2:13).

"Let us fix our eyes on Jesus, the *author* and *perfecter* of our faith..." (Hebrews 12:2, author's emphasis). It is the Lord who first reached out to begin the relationship, and it is He who will complete it.

In essence, when we understand that God's love is the foundation for our relationship with Him, we've come full circle. We need to be in relationship with God, but the only way we can be in that relationship is because of what He has done for us.

It is God's grace and love that establish us in that relationship initially, and it is also His love and mercy that cause that relationship to be ongoing. It all begins and ends with His grace. "He who began a good work in you will carry it on to completion until the day of Christ Jesus" (Philippians 1:6).

It is because of the everlasting love of the Lord that our relationship with Him is a settled issue. There is no need to wonder whether God loves you ("Can I really have a relationship with Almighty

God?"). Jesus' atoning work on the cross proves His love once and for all.

One of the earliest glimpses in the Bible of God's heart is right after Adam sinned. "But the LORD God called to the man, 'Where are you?'" (Genesis 3:9). This picture of the loving Father in search of His lost child is the underlying theme of all of Scripture. The main message throughout the Bible is that God loves us. If we see Him as the evil taskmaster waiting to beat us when we do wrong, we have not understood His care for us. "God *is* love" (1 John 4:16, author's emphasis).

Regardless of how long we have walked with the Lord, there is something refreshing about receiving God's love anew. One of my favorite present-day songwriters is Mark Altrogge. One of his songs, "The Love of a Holy God," says this, "I'm ruined for this world for I've tasted Your love, the love of a holy God." The fact that God is so holy and yet still loves sinful creatures like us makes His love even more wonderful. All the treasures of this world pale in comparison.

This matter of God's love and grace is the foundation on which we must build our entire lives. We must stop trying to earn God's favor and recognize the reality of what His love and grace have already done for us. "Therefore, there is now *no condemnation* for those who are in Christ Jesus, because through Christ Jesus the law of the Spirit of life set me free from the law of sin and death" (Romans 8:1-2, author's emphasis).

No matter how good you or I ever become, there is still only one foundation: the love and grace of God in the form of the blood of Jesus shed for the forgiveness of our sins in order to make us acceptable to God. In reality, all the rest are just peripheral issues.

The very final words that God chose to end His written message to mankind reemphasize the point: "The grace of the Lord Jesus be with God's people. Amen" (Revelation 22:21).

If all that we do in life is not built on the foundation of His love, then the structure will never be solid. We are all simply sinners saved by the immeasurable grace and sacrifice of the Lord Jesus.

"Because of the LORD's great love we are not consumed, for His compassions never fail. They are new every morning; great is Your faithfulness" (Lamentations 3:22-23).

Personal application:

1. Is your relationship with God built solidly on the foundation of His love? If not, reread chapters 6-12 and mark the sections that speak to your situation.

2. Take time right now to thank the Lord that He is at work in your life. It is He who will ultimately cause you to become more like Himself.

Part 3

Obstacles to Our Relationship With God

There are sometimes things that can be obstacles to our relationship with God. Situations in our lives can occasionally become a hindrance to our fellowship with Him.

I know if I were to sit down with you and discuss this idea, you could easily list several different issues that you struggle with in this area. We all have them. However, beyond each of our individual struggles, there are also other concerns that are fairly universal, concerns to which nearly any Christian can relate.

The following chapters will pinpoint a few of these obstacles and offer help in avoiding them.

e, and Idolater?!?

Quite some time ago I heard a man make a very strong statement. He said, "If I meet someone for the first time and I allow him to guide the conversation, I'll know within 10 or 15 minutes who or what his god is because we talk about that which is most important to us." This statement is a generalization, but in general it is true. The things that are the most important to us get the most time on our lips.

Many years ago I had an album (you know, those black vinyl disks that were played on a record player) by the music group Dogwood. One song in particular, "Remember the Rebels," really pierced me. It was about the idol that King Nebuchadnezzar had built and how Shadrach, Meshach, and Abednego refused to bow down to it, so the king had them thrown into the fiery furnace (Daniel 3:1-30). The song told the story and then, to make the point, suggested that an idol could be almost anything, "From a treasured reputation to a childhood dream." The song went on to say that the fire we may experience in our own lives may not be fire of sulphur and ashes at all. More likely it is simply the pain of giving the idol up.

It's so easy for things to creep into our lives and become more important to us than God. And anything that does become more important to us than God has then become an idol.

The prophet Ezekiel saw a vision that is recorded in Ezekiel 44. In that vision the Lord said He was banishing the Levites from ministering before Him. He told them that they would still be allowed to "slaughter the burnt offerings and sacrifices for the people and stand before the people and serve them" and to perform "the duties of the temple and all the work that is to be done in it" (Ezekiel 44:11, 14). However, they would no longer be able to come near to God and minister to Him. They had apparently done something that had caused the Lord to become angry with them.

Obviously, this is a historical passage of Scripture and cannot be used to draw a universal, all-encompassing truth. However, in reading a passage like this, it seems apparent that there is a lesson from which we can learn. God is telling these Levites that they can still minister to the people and they can still do the work of the temple, but they will no longer be allowed to come before Him. As a child of God, I want to know what it is that they did that caused the Lord to have such a reaction. Why? Because I want to live as far away from those things as I possibly can. I have no desire for God to banish me from His presence.

In reading the full context of this passage of Scripture (Ezekiel 44:4-14), there is a very clearly stated reason for God's reaction: Verses 10 and 12 both indicate that the Levites had worshiped idols.

The Lord had explicitly told the entire nation of Israel in the very first commandment: "You shall have no other gods before Me"

(Exodus 20:3). Beyond the commitment of the rest of Israel, the Levites were to be dedicated *totally* to God (Numbers 8:14-16). This was their lot in life. Because they willfully violated God's commandment, the Lord banished them from His presence.

It is all too easy for us to allow those idols in our lives, also. Not consciously, of course. You and I do not have idols of wood or stone to which we bow down (at least I hope not!). However, as stated earlier, practically anything can become an idol. When we relegate anything in our lives to a higher place than God, that thing has become an idol.

Earlier in this book I mentioned the rich young ruler who came to Jesus inquiring about what he must do to inherit eternal life. At the end of that scenario, the young man leaves and is very sad "because he had great wealth" (Mark 10:22). His money had become his god. Anything that becomes more important to us than the Lord—anything that displaces our relationship with Him—is an idol.

Sometimes I find it necessary to pray, not in some sort of gross, introspective way, but in humility and sincerity, "Lord, are there any idols in my life? Because if there are, I want to know about them and deal with them, because I want You to always have first place in my life." Each of us, from time to time, would do well to pray that prayer.

Our relationship with God is our number one priority, and there are a myriad of things that seem to want to distract us from that priority. In your life, do not let any idols pull you away from what is most important.

Personal application:

1. When you meet someone for the first time, what do you usually talk about most? (Your accomplishments, your children, your job, your dreams in life, etc.) Is this an indication of what is really "god" in your life? If so, perhaps now would be a good time to confess and repent.

2. Make a point of periodically asking the Lord to show you if there are any idols in your life.

Chapter 14

raffiti on the Temple Walls

Have you ever walked into a worship service and thought (or said) something negative about a brother or sister in Christ? Perhaps something like, "There's Joe. I wish he'd grow up, get his hair cut, and act like a normal Christian." Or, "There's Sue. I hope she doesn't start telling me any of those things she thinks God is telling her. I don't think He's telling her any of those things. I think she's just weird."

Have you ever walked into a worship service and thought (or said)...something like, "There's Joe. I wish he's grow up, get his hair cut, and act like a normal Christian."

Have you ever done that or anything like that? And if you have, what was the outcome? You put a wall between yourself and that person. Our negative attitudes toward one another will hinder our relationship with God.

In the second chapter of his letter to the believers in Ephesus, Paul discusses the concept of the Church being built together into a holy temple. He concludes this section with these words. "And in Him you too are being built together to become a dwelling in which God lives by His Spirit" (Ephesians 2:22).

For most Christians this idea is not new. The concept that God is building us together into a building, into a temple, is a foundational teaching of the Church. It is found in both the Old and New Testaments. To me this is so fundamental that I would consider it a part of "Basic Christianity 101."

Yet even when we understand that God is indeed building us together, we often miss His purpose in doing it. Why is He making us into a building?

The answer is found in the second chapter of Peter's first epistle. "You also, like living stones, are being built into a spiritual house *to be a holy priesthood, offering spiritual sacrifices acceptable to God through Jesus Christ*" (1 Peter 2:5, author's emphasis). As believers in Jesus, we have become the New Testament priesthood. Our lives are to be given wholly to the Lord, just like the Old Testament priests. Being that "holy priesthood offering spiritual sacrifices" is a big part of our relationship with Him.

Ultimately, according to Peter, that is what we are all about. The reason that God is building us together into a building is that we might more fully be in relationship with Him.

If this is true (and obviously Scripture says it is), then it follows logically that if the building is not built properly, then our spiritual sacrifices will be lacking. If our relationships with one another are out of order, then the purpose of the building will not be fulfilled.

Paul phrased it like this: "Don't you know that you yourselves are God's temple and that God's Spirit lives in you? If anyone destroys God's temple, God will destroy him; for God's temple is sacred, and you (plural) are that temple" (1 Corinthians 3:16-17).

The Greek word here for destroying the temple literally means to "corrupt" or to "mar." In Bible times if anyone was caught doing any type of damage to the temple—writing graffiti on the walls for example—there was an instant death sentence pronounced. If you were caught, there was no question in anyone's mind what the outcome would be. Your life was over.

However, we do that very thing when we come to church harboring negative attitudes toward our brothers and sisters in Christ. We are corrupting, marring, destroying the temple into which the Lord is building us. Even if this is not our intent, we can unknowingly destroy the temple by harboring resentments and other negative attitudes toward others.

I am not trying to say that we should have extremely close relationships with everyone we know. This is impossible. There are various levels of relationships. We can see this even in the life of Jesus. He had the multitudes that followed Him. From the multitudes He had seventy-two followers that He appointed and sent out two by two (Luke 10:1-20). From among these He chose twelve apostles. Of these, Jesus seemed to have an "inner circle" of three—Peter, James, and John—who were nearly always with Him. And even from these three the Bible frequently refers to John as the disciple "Jesus loved," suggesting a special relationship between Jesus and John. Obviously, we too, have various levels of relationships.

It is important for us to understand the nature of relationships, but there is also a danger for us in understanding it. We can begin to view some relationships as unimportant. Be honest. Are there certain people in the Body of Christ you have difficulty relating to? Are there some folks with whom you even avoid making eye contact in order to keep from talking with them?

After many years as a Christian, I finally came to the realization that on this side of eternity I would never see eye to eye with everyone in the kingdom. The truth is that being in complete agreement is of very little consequence. What really matters is that I understand that Jesus paid just as much for those people I do not fully agree with as He did for me. This mindset quickly changes my perspective on people. I make the choice to walk in love and unity with my brothers and sisters in the Lord.

> **Holding unforgiveness in our hearts will sever our relationship with God...that's much too high a price to pay.**

Jesus stressed the importance of our relationships with the Body of Christ. He said, "Therefore, if you are offering your gift at the altar and there remember that your brother has something against you, leave your gift there in front of the altar. First go and be reconciled to your brother; then come and offer your gift" (Matthew 5:23-24).

This principle can also be seen clearly in Jesus' words immediately following His sharing of the Lord's Prayer. "But if you do not forgive men their sins, your Father will not forgive your sins" (Matthew 6:15). Holding unforgiveness in our hearts will sever our relationship with God...that's much too high a price to pay.

When we harbor negative attitudes toward fellow-Christians, it will greatly hinder our relationship with God.

Personal application:

1. Who are the people you avoid on Sunday morning? Are you entertaining negative thoughts about them that are hindering your relationship with God? (If yes, go back to the chapters on repentance and forgiveness and take care of business.) Do you have some graffiti to erase on the Temple walls?

Chapter 15

Proper Perspective in Problems

everal years ago I went through a particularly trying ordeal. Seemingly, my entire world was turned upside down in a brief period of time. In the midst of this scenario I wondered where God was. I questioned why He seemed silent and uncaring. For a time, my relationship with the Lord suffered because of the difficult situation through which I was walking.

Perhaps you, too, have encountered such a scenario in your life. Going through difficult situations can sometimes cause struggles in our relationship with the Lord. Knowing how to walk confidently *through* these times can be the key to maintaining that strong relationship with God.

During the time of David, Asaph was a prophet, a musician, and a leader among God's people. In Psalm 73, Asaph is reflecting back on a very trying time he had gone through. "Surely God is good to Israel, to those who are pure in heart. But as for me, my feet had almost slipped; I had nearly lost my foothold. For I envied the arrogant when I saw the prosperity of the wicked" (Psalm 73:1-3).

Asaph saw around him those who did not know God. These people apparently did not even care about God, and they were doing better financially than he was doing. As a result he became obviously distraught about this scenario.

Over the next several verses Asaph laments the situation. Read these verses with a whine: "This is what the wicked are like—always carefree, they increase in wealth. Surely in vain have I kept my heart pure; in vain have I washed my hands in innocence. All day long I have been plagued; I have been punished every morning" (Psalm 73:12-14).

Can you hear the lament? He is having a pity party. We can scoff or even laugh at his words, but if you have ever been in a similar situation, you understand that this is reality for Asaph. This is not a joke. This is a very difficult time in his life.

Finally something happens that changes his perspective. "When I tried to understand all this, it was oppressive to me till I entered the sanctuary of God; then I understood their final destiny" (Psalm 73:16-17).

It seems that suddenly Asaph began to understand what the Apostle James said in his letter to God's people. "What is your life? You are a mist that appears for a little while and then vanishes" (James 4:14). Asaph started to realize that this life is not all there is. We're just here for a little while. Heaven is our real home. We are just aliens here. We have our papers to work here for a while, but this is not really our home. Heaven is. The Apostle Paul said it this way, "If only for this life we have hope in Christ, we are to be pitied more than all men" (1 Corinthians 15:19). There is more to life than just this life. "For our light and momentary troubles are achieving for us an eternal glory that far outweighs them all" (2 Corinthians 4:17). "I consider that our present sufferings are not worth comparing with the glory that will be revealed in us" (Romans 8:18).

Please understand that we may have some great blessings here in this life. However, if we gain the heavenly perspective of the Apostle Paul, we will find the difficult times much easier to walk through. This is exactly what happened to Asaph.

I have found that anytime we find ourselves in a difficult situation, two things are always constant. One is the problem itself. It might be a lie from the enemy, but to you it is as big as life, staring you in the face. The other thing that is always constant is that God is on His throne. The Creator/Redeemer is still sovereign. We choose which of these two we will look at. We can look at the problem, or we can look at the One who is able to carry us through the problem. "David said about Him: 'I saw the Lord always before me. Because He is at my right hand, I will not be shaken'" (Acts 2:25).

> **We can look at the problem, or we can look at the One who is able to carry us through the problem.**

When we begin to get things in their proper perspective, the situation seems much more manageable. When we realize that regardless of what it looks like on the surface God is still in control, it makes life easier to face. As we understand that heaven is a real place and that we are going there one day, suddenly the trials of this life pale in comparison.

In Asaph's story in Psalm 73, it is very likely that nothing in the natural changed. The wicked people were still prospering, and Asaph was still in his same financial condition. But he now understood their prosperity was only temporal and that he had treasures stored up for him in heavenly places (Matthew 6:19, 20). What changed was Asaph's heart, and when that happens everything changes.

Look at some of the verses that follow.

> Surely You place them on slippery ground; You cast them down to ruin. How suddenly are they destroyed, completely swept away by terrors! As a dream when one awakes, so when You arise, O Lord, You will despise them as fantasies. When my heart was

grieved and my spirit embittered, I was senseless and ignorant; I was a brute beast before You. Yet I am always with You; You hold me by my right hand. You guide me with Your counsel, and afterward You will take me into glory. Whom have I in heaven but You? And earth has nothing I desire besides You. My flesh and my heart may fail, but God is the strength of my heart and my portion forever (Psalm 73:18-26).

Does this sound like the same man? In just a few short sentences he has done a 180 degree turnaround simply by gaining God's perspective on the situation. Someone once said that gaining God's perspective totally rearranges our lives.

Realizing, first of all, that this life is not all there is to life, and second, that regardless of the situation, God is still in control, makes maintaining our relationship with Him during difficult times much easier. Earthly trials can make heavenly treasures more real. When we are going through struggles, our relationship with God can be sweeter if we keep our focus on Him.

Personal application:

1. When problems come, which do you usually look at—the problem or the One Who is in control?

2. When Asaph "entered the sanctuary of God," his perspective on his problems changed. Practically speaking, how do you or how can you also "enter the sanctuary" when you face problems?

3. The next time you're facing a problem (maybe that's right now), why not compose your own psalm focusing on the Solution?

Chapter 16

How Can I Worship? I'm in the Wrong Pew!

Not long ago I ministered at a church where some renovation had recently taken place. Some things were changed in the sanctuary that necessitated removing a few sections of pews. Unfortunately, that meant the people who normally sat in those pews had to find new seats. One of the pastors of the church told me those who had been displaced had a difficult time readjusting. They (and their families) had been accustomed to sitting in those particular (now removed) pews for years.

Having a particular place set aside for congregational and/or personal worship can be of great benefit to fully and regularly entering in to worship. Too often, like the people I described above, we become so location oriented that unless we are in what we believe to be a "holy spot" (often a church building or even a particular place within a church building), we find ourselves unable to worship or be in relationship with God. This concept is in direct opposition to a true Scriptural understanding of worship and relationship with God.

In the fourth chapter of the Gospel of John, Jesus is talking with the Samaritan woman. During their conversation Jesus touches a little too close to home for her, and she quickly changes the subject. As usual, Jesus is completely unfazed by her tactic. He simply picks up the conversation where she has directed it.

"Our fathers worshiped on this mountain, but you Jews claim that the place where we must worship is in Jerusalem."

Jesus declared, "Believe me, woman, a time is coming when you will worship the Father neither on this mountain nor in Jerusalem. You Samaritans worship what you do not know; we worship what we do know, for salvation is from the Jews. Yet a time is coming and has now come when the true worshipers will worship the Father in spirit and truth, for they are the kind of worshipers the Father seeks. God is Spirit, and His worshipers must worship in spirit and in truth" (John 4:20-24).

In this section of Scripture, Jesus once and for all lays to rest the notion that God is limited to a particular place. He is clearly telling us that the location is unimportant. God is a Spirit, and we can be in relationship with Him anywhere and everywhere.

Unfortunately, this is completely contrary to our normal way of thinking. Most people have the idea that the church building is the only place for fellowship with God.* Many of us even sit in exactly the same place in the building from week to week. In fact, most of

---

*I am not suggesting to neglect the corporate gathering of the saints. Scripture is very clear that we should gather together with God's people. Hebrews 10:25 says, "Let us not give up meeting together, as some are in the habit of doing..."

us have difficulty concentrating on the service if our "spot" is taken and we are forced to sit somewhere else. This is, at least in part, because we are such creatures of habit.

As I travel I repeatedly hear stories of people who are asked to move because they are seated in someone else's normal spot for Sunday-morning worship. I thought this was just a cultural quirk. However, some time ago I was ministering in a church in Poland where the people had their own cushions on the pews, marking their spots from week to week. (I wanted to move the cushions around just to shake the people up a bit.) We can all become so accustomed to the same place that we have difficulty adjusting to a different one.

Perhaps an illustration from Dr. Judson Cornwall will help me make the point. Did you know that the Holy Spirit got lost on the day of Pentecost? Okay, He probably did not, but it is a good story.

Up until the time of Pentecost, God chose to manifest Himself in a particular place. It was on the holy mountain, at Moses' tabernacle, in Solomon's temple, etc. It was always in a specific place. On the day of Pentecost, the Holy Spirit was on His way to the temple, took a wrong turn, ended up in the upper room and filled everyone there. And from that point on, the Bible never speaks of a holy place. It talks about a holy people. We, the Church, are that holy people. Since the day of Pentecost, God has chosen to dwell not in a particular geographic location but in His people.

"For *we* are the temple of the living God" (2 Corinthians 6:16b, author's emphasis). "Don't you know that you yourselves are God's temple and that God's Spirit lives in you?" (1 Corinthians 3:16).

Ultimately, then, it really should not matter where we are geographically. Because we are the temple we can worship and be in fellowship with God in any location in which we find ourselves.

I sometimes go grocery shopping with my wife. Actually she does the shopping; I have the mindless job of pushing the cart. Often, while walking up and down the aisles pushing the grocery cart, I sing praises to the Lord. I try not to be loud or obnoxious about it, but I am convinced that God is just as worthy in the marketplace on Thursday night as He is in the church building on Sunday morning.

We must begin to realize more fully that the church building where we corporately gather is not the temple. We are. And because of this truth we can fellowship with and worship the Lord anywhere.

Personal application:

1. Do you feel you need to be in a church building in order to worship or relate to God?

2. Name at least three other places where you could be fellowshiping with God.

3. If it is not the place that matters in worship, what are the essential components of true worship?

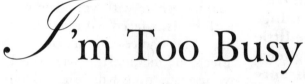I'm Too Busy

Recently I flew out of the airport at Salt Lake City, Utah. As we ascended I noticed that at a certain altitude the air suddenly became clear. I hadn't even noticed the bluish-gray haze until we passed out of it. Once above the fog everything was much more vivid. The mountaintops, the sky, the sun, all took on a far more intense quality. I was honestly rather startled because, as I mentioned, I had not even realized that there was a haze obscuring these things.

Sometimes the busyness of life can blur our vision. Little things and sometimes big things can creep in, and we don't even notice that we have become dulled to the things of God.

Most Christians, when they *honestly* look at their schedules, find that they spend way too much time doing things that have little or no long-term significance

One of the most potent obstacles in our relationship with God is just that: the busyness of everyday life. Although I alluded to this in an earlier chapter, it seems to me to be significant enough to spend further time addressing it.

There is no way to soft-pedal what I'm about to share with you. The reality is that each of us is faced with choices every single day. The choices we make will ultimately affect our relationship with the Lord. How we use our time will bring us into a closer walk with God or will distance us from Him.

In his book *Building High Commitment in a Low Commitment World*, Bill Hull says this:

> When a person says, "I am too busy to make a commitment to spiritual growth or service," my return shot is, "Let's take a look at your schedule." In almost every case I have found that the person has found time for golf, attendance at sporting events, and other fun activities. I believe that people need recreational activity and other ways to relax, but they also spend hours watching television and waste even more time in unproductive activity that could be delegated. When they sit down and actually see how much discretionary time they have, it is embarrassing and shocking, but hopeful.[1]

It's true. Most Christians, when they *honestly* look at their schedules, find that they spend way too much time doing things that have little or no long-term significance.

Part of the problem today is that we are faced with so many choices in life. At the time of Jesus, the number of options for any leisure time the people had were severely limited. Even in this country as recently as fifty years ago, the possibilities of things to do with spare time were certainly nowhere close to what face us today.

Noted author and speaker Os Guinness said it like this:

The modern world offers an endless range of choice and change, overwhelming traditional simplicities and cohesion. Crowded modern cities mean that we are all much closer, yet stranger, to each other. The modern explosion of knowledge means that people, places, periods, and psyches are accessible as never before...Modern travel whistles us to any part of the world. Modern media brings us the world and its dazzling array of options at the push of a button. Modern business makes the products of the world available in our neighborhoods.

This intensification of choice and change has effects on many levels. The heightened awareness of the presence of others increases our awareness of possibilities for ourselves. *Their* cuisines, *their* customs, *their* convictions can become *our* choices, *our* options, *our* possibilities. Life has become a smorgasbord with an endless array of dishes.[2]

That endless array of choices can be a good thing. However, it can also be a bad thing. Guinness goes on to say this:

And more important still, choice is no longer just a state of mind. Choice has become a value, a priority, a right...

To many people, choice has become a god. Don't try to take away our choices! We like having all of those possibilities. Don't try to force us make long-term commitments. We want to "keep our options open."

Bill Hull states it even more directly:

Choice has been given a place above self-discipline, self-denial, honesty and faithfulness...This has led to the abandonment of the standard expectations that everyone should practice the same set of spiritual habits such as Bible reading, prayer, stewardship, service, accountability, etc. Therefore, spirituality becomes self-directed, and being spiritual becomes whatever each individual chooses to make it. This leads to superficial Christianity. The only road to spiritual depth and maturity is a road of consistency and self-discipline.[3]

I really don't want you to dislike me for limiting your options. However, Jesus Himself said, "If anyone would come after Me, he must deny himself and take up his cross and follow Me" (Matthew 16:24; Mark 8:34; Luke 9:23). To "deny" one's self means to eliminate some of the extracurricular options. Too often we have bowed our knees to the god of Choice instead of denying ourselves.

The busyness of our day—the endless array of choices—must be limited. We must ask ourselves, what are the things that are of *real* significance? If I never experience the many options that are calling for my attention, will it make any eternal difference?

In just a few chapters we will be discussing the practical how-to's of relationship with the Lord, what we *should* be doing. It seems to me, though, that eliminating what we *shouldn't* be doing can be just as important.

Let me offer a practical thought from my own life. Nearly fifteen years ago my wife and I made the decision that we would not have television in our home. We did not want the influence in our lives nor the time wasted staring blankly at a show of little or no positive value. It was a choice that has paid very positive dividends for our family life and our spiritual life.

Am I telling you to get rid of your television? No. I am telling you, however, that the decisions you make will affect your spiritual life. Someone once said, "Anything less than a conscious commitment to the important is an unconscious commitment to the unimportant."

I find it interesting to note that when Jesus told the parable of the sower, He made reference to seed that fell among thorns (Mark 4:3-20). He explained to His disciples that the thorns included chasing after all the things this world has to offer. I had read this parable a gazillion times in the past, and I always thought that the thorns had choked and killed the plant. As I recently read the parable again, I realized that the plant had not died. The thorns simply choked it and made it unfruitful. The plant was still alive, but there was not enough life left in it to bear fruit. Pursuing the endless array of what this world offers can make our lives unfruitful also.

Perhaps you need to evaluate what things you are doing that are hindering your relationship with God.

Even as I write this, though, I can hear the cries of despair: "But you don't understand my situation. Knowing the Lord takes time, and time is something I just don't have!"

I can definitely empathize with this thought. It is all too easy for me also to put aside the things that I say are of the greatest value:

prayer, Bible study, personal worship, communion with God. All of the disciplines by which I can know God better are often pushed aside until a more convenient time.

Now is the time. Regardless of what it takes, this is the key for us in this hour: seek God. There is no longer time for life as usual. We must reprioritize our lives and make choices with our time that will have long-term value.

Personal application:

1. Honestly look at your schedule. Are there things of little or no long-term consequence that you should eliminate to make more time for God?

2. Choose one thing this week and delete it from your schedule. Instead, use the time to strengthen your relationship with the Lord.

3. What does it mean for you where you are right now in your walk with God to "deny (yourself) and take up (your) cross and follow (Christ)"?

Chapter 18

Don't Forget: Love Jesus Every Day!

For a couple of years my wife was a part of a women's Bible study with participants from dozens of churches. One day, in a small group setting, one of the ladies shared about her teenage son. She stated that she was very glad he chose to listen to a particular secular radio station and a specific deejay. The reason for his choice was that that announcer did not use as much profanity and was not quite

109

as vulgar as many of the others. The mom sharing this thought it was great that her son had made such a wise choice on his own.

When my wife shared the incident with me, my mental reaction was immediate. "We have reached a point where we think that a little profanity and a less-than-usual amount of vulgarity is good. How outrageous!"

Paul wrote to Timothy about people "whose consciences have been seared as with a hot iron" (1 Timothy 4:2b). The truth is that this type of person is fairly common in our society.

I remember part of a sermon I heard as a young man. The pastor was relating several Scriptures, but then, to emphasize his point, he shared an old Indian proverb. "Conscience is like a three-pointed stone inside of a man. The more he goes against his conscience, the more the points wear off the stone." The pastor went on to explain that eventually, if we violate our conscience often enough, it will no longer affect us.

Our culture makes violating our conscience extremely easy. We are constantly bombarded with audio and video images that are far below the Scriptural standard of "whatever is true, whatever is noble, whatever is right, whatever is pure, whatever is lovely, whatever is admirable—if anything is excellent or praiseworthy—think about such things" (Philippians 4:8). This ongoing assault can eventually wear down even those who are strong.

Those images will lead us away from the path that is highest. That's their goal. If they can keep our attention drawn toward those things that are in opposition to God, then they will always have an audience.

Nearly all advertisements and much of the television, movie, and radio industries will ultimately lead us down a path contrary to God's holiness. They use as a basis those enticements that are in direct opposition to the Lord: the lust of the eyes, the lust of the flesh, and the pride of life. "Get this product and you'll be fulfilled." "Check out this awesome body." "One little taste won't hurt anything." "Go ahead, you deserve it." And on and on and on. All very cleverly devised to pull us off the course of pursuing our goal of being in close, intimate relationship with the Lord.

When I encounter quotes and ideas that I consider especially profound, I generally endeavor to make a note of them.

Unfortunately, some time ago I copied a quote from a magazine article but completely missed getting the source information. I do not like using quotes without giving the reference, but this one is so appropriate I decided to make an exception.

> We must be absolutely intolerant of the cultural compromises foisted on us by contemporary materialistic Western Christianity. Instead, one must search the Scriptures; seek the Holy Spirit; ask "Where have the insidious tentacles of materialism gripped my soul? Where am I beginning to die at the edges?"

What a mouthful. Have you been affected by the insidious tentacles of materialism? Are you always absolutely intolerant of cultural compromises? The Apostle Paul phrased it like this: "Put to death, therefore, whatever belongs to your earthly nature..." (Colossians 3:5). This is not a passive statement. You cannot put a part of your earthly nature to death with a ho-hum attitude.

Perhaps one of the best ways to overcome being tainted by our culture is through fellowship with one another. "But encourage one another daily, as long as it is called Today, so that none of you may be hardened by sin's deceitfulness" (Hebrews 3:13). Would you like to keep from being hardened by sin's deceitfulness? Then you need encouragement from your brothers and sisters in Christ.

...little two-year-old Amy looked up at me and said, "Daddy, don't *you* forget: love Jesus every day."

A few years ago I inadvertently added something to my little girl's bedtime routine. After our usual singing and praying, while I was tucking her in, I said, "Amy, don't forget: love Jesus every day." I liked the concept so much that I said it the next night and the next. After about a week of doing this, I received a very unexpected response. As I again tucked her into bed and told her to love Jesus every day, little two-year-old Amy looked up at me and said, "Daddy, don't *you* forget: love Jesus every day." I looked at her, a bit misty-eyed, and, with a little catch in my voice, I responded, "Thanks for reminding me, Amy. Sometimes I need to hear that." The truth is that we all do. As Hebrews 3:13 tells us, regular encouragement from brothers and sisters in Christ will indeed keep us from being tainted by the deceitfulness of sin. We all need to be consistently encouraged to continue on in our walk with Jesus.

That consistent encouragement is one of the best ways to keep from becoming hardened by the deceptiveness of our sinful society.

Personal application:

1. Does your daily/weekly routine expose the "insidious tentacles of materialism"? If yes, what are you doing to free yourself from their influence?

2. What are two ways you can encourage specific people you care about to love Jesus every day?

3. What habits do you have or can you develop to encourage yourself to love Jesus every day?

$\mathcal{F}$amiliarity Breeds Contempt (Or At Least Boredom)

$\mathcal{A}$ few years ago a friend of mine began sharing some of the frustrations he had with his life. As a college-age believer, he had always been full of zeal and enthusiasm for the things of God. Now, as a married thirty-something father of four, he realized that his fervor had waned drastically. He looked around our congregation and saw people who reminded him of the fervor of his younger days. My friend had not consciously abandoned his passion for the Lord. It simply slipped away over time.

One of the major problems that marriage counselors encounter dealing with married couples is that of familiarity. The two people who were once completely enamored with each other have become accustomed to one another. The old adage that "familiarity breeds contempt" becomes all too real. The original spark is gone. Boredom sets in.

In any marriage, if the partners do not cultivate the seeds of a good relationship, over time the relationship dies. Whereas they once saw only good things in each other, they eventually lose sight of the very things that once attracted them to one another. Eventually, the simple caring gestures and loving attitudes that strengthened their relationship disappear. Neglect and indifference replace them. The posture of giving and genuine concern for the other fades and is supplanted by apathy.

Unfortunately, just like my friend's experience, much the same thing often happens in our relationship with the Lord. If we do not cultivate our relationship with God, it will wither. Over a period of time our love for our Redeemer can fade.

Just like King Amaziah who did the right things halfheartedly (2 Chronicles 25:1-28), it is all too easy for us to become lackadaisical. We may even go through the motions, but there is no life in it. We can become overly accustomed to God and His actions. We too often take Him and what He does for granted.

Our spiritual life needs consistent maintenance just to stay level. If we expect to grow spiritually, it needs even more work.

Recently, I was contemplating the lives of some of the great men and women of God of this past century. Some of their exploits were tremendous. At their hands, thousands of people were restored to physical and mental health. Tens of thousands came into the kingdom through their preaching of the Word. Countless people heard the truth of God's Word proclaimed and were affected by it for the first time.

However, I was amazed to find that nearly half of the people that I had looked at ended up "fizzling out" toward the end of their lives. They either lost all intensity or seemingly turned away from God altogether. The great deeds they did in the Name of Jesus were just distant memories from their past.

That's the bad news. The good news is that over half of those I studied had maintained a zeal and a fervency for God. They never lost their passion for the Lord and continued influencing their world until they passed on into glory. If that speaks nothing else to us, it should say that it is possible to live our entire lives zealously for the Lord.

Romans 12:11 tells us, "Never be lacking in zeal, but keep your spiritual fervor, serving the Lord." Although most of us would give verbal assent to the necessity of doing this, the truth is that the church in America is sadly lacking in zeal and fervency. Like some of those amazing men and women of God whose lives I examined, we often seem to have lost our passion for the Lord.

Not long ago I heard a man make a statement that caused me to reflect. He said that a Laodicean spirit has come upon the church in America. He was referring to the Lord's indictment against the church of Laodicea in the book of Revelation: "I know your deeds, that you are neither cold nor hot. I wish you were either one or the other! So, because you are lukewarm—neither hot nor cold—I am about to spit you out of My mouth. You say, 'I am rich; I have acquired wealth and do not need a thing.' But you do not realize that you are wretched, pitiful, poor, blind and naked. I counsel you to buy from Me gold refined in the fire, so you can become rich; and white clothes to wear, so you can cover your shameful nakedness; and salve to put on your eyes, so you can see" (Revelation 3:15-18).

Unfortunately, I would agree with this man's assessment of the North American church. We have more seminars, conferences, books, tapes, schools, and churches than any other nation, but we are producing what appears to be the least fervent brand of Christianity on earth. There is little or no zeal in most Christians, except, of course, sometimes on Sunday mornings. The Bible does not teach that we should be zealous only on Sunday mornings. It says that we are never to be lacking in zeal. For most Christians in our country, godly zeal is a foreign concept.

The ongoing reports of the enthusiasm of the church in other areas of the world, especially Asia and Africa, are inspiring to me. There are churches in Asia and Africa growing by thousands per day because of the zeal of the church. Often the genuine fervor of Christians in other nations puts us to shame.

The reality is that there is nothing more inherently evil in us as a nation than other nations. The problem is that we have known God longer than many. And with that knowing has come complacency. It almost seems to be a natural human tendency.

In his thought-provoking book *Fresh Wind, Fresh Fire*, Jim said it like this:

> Isn't it remarkable that only two of the seven churches of Revelation (Pergamum and Thyatira) were scolded for false doctrine? Far more common was a lack of spiritual vitality, of fervency, of closeness to the Lord. These are what the glorified Christ wanted to talk about most.[3]

Often we look at the people of Israel in the Bible and wonder how they could possibly be so stupid. They had seen the Red Sea parted and the great army of Egypt swallowed by its waters. This was not coincidence. They had actually seen a bona fide miracle. Yet not much later they decided they needed a golden calf to be their god. How could that be? Remember, this is only one incident out of hundreds that often leave us scratching our heads and wondering what was wrong with them.

Unfortunately, without realizing it we, too, often act the same way. We become so accustomed to the grace and mercy of God that we take them for granted. We get so used to His actions that we frequently miss them completely.

As new believers we often trust God for everything. After a while, however, we begin to trust more in ourselves than in Him and His faithfulness. We take Him for granted. Also, as baby Christians we are usually exuberant in our thankfulness and praise to Him. Unfortunately, this zeal in honoring God frequently fades with the passing of time.

Allow me to pose a question or two. Because we have known the Lord for a longer time is He now less trustworthy? Is He less worthy of our praise? Of course not. If anything, we have probably seen the faithfulness of our God again and again during our walk with Him.

So what's the answer? First, we must recognize the problem. The main thing, though, is the point of this whole book: cultivate and maintain our relationship with the Lord. Just like married couples who become accustomed to each other, we, too, can become overly familiar with God and His ways. We must see the necessity of cultivating a God-consciousness in our lives. Strengthening our relationship with Him must become an absolute priority.

Personal application:

1. What miracles has God done in your life that you would do well to remember? It might be good to begin with the greatest miracle of all: He brought you out of darkness into His wonderful light (1 Peter 2:9b).

2. Keep a list this week of ways God works in your life. Name as many and be as specific as you can.

3. Pray for a fresh realization in your mind and heart of the living God within you.

$\mathscr{B}$reaking Heartless Habits

$\mathscr{H}$ave you ever seen either a stage or movie production of the play "Fiddler on the Roof"? One song in that production drives home an interesting point. In response to why the people do certain things that they do, the song simply repeats over and over, "Tradition."

The reality of life is that we humans are often creatures of habit. We do the same things over and over, not because it is really heart-felt, but simply because it is habit.

Not only can the whole of God's work in us become "old hat," but our very actions that once helped us know Him can become heartless habits. This section applies mostly to the corporate church setting, but it also has application to individual relationships with the Lord. Some people seem to have great difficulty worshiping the Lord if the order of service is changed or rearranged. We are comfortable with our traditions and we do not like change. This is simply human nature.

There is ultimately nothing wrong with order. God is obviously portrayed as a God of order throughout Scripture. The Bible even specifically tells us that everything should be done in a fitting and orderly way (1 Corinthians 14:40). The problem comes in when we substitute the actions themselves for that in which God is really interested: our hearts.

Through the prophet Isaiah, God lambastes His chosen people, Israel. He starts off by referring to them as "rulers of Sodom" and "people of Gomorrah." He is obviously not very happy with them! What have they done to deserve such a tirade? Listen to His words:

"The multitude of your sacrifices—what are they to Me?" says the LORD. "I have more than enough of burnt offerings, of rams and the fat of fattened animals; I have no pleasure in the blood of bulls and lambs and goats. When you come to appear before Me, who has asked this of you, this trampling of My courts? Stop bringing meaningless offerings! Your incense is detestable to Me. New Moons, Sabbaths and convocations—I cannot bear your evil assemblies. Your New Moon festivals and your appointed feasts My soul hates. They have become a burden to Me; I am weary of bearing them" (Isaiah 1:11-14).

Does this section of Scripture seem a bit strange to you? It was, after all, God who had asked for all of these things in the first place. He was the One who had requested the sacrifices. It was God who had asked for the burnt offerings, the festivals, the incense, and the feasts. And now He emphatically tells them to stop.

The real issue was not the practices themselves. It was the people's hearts. Once again, by this point in the history of Israel, God was certainly not unhappy with their outward manners on these issues. Israel had become very adept at all of these. In fact, with their years of practice, they were probably so good at performing these rituals that they could do any or all of them without even thinking about them. That was the problem. They were going through the motions, but there was no real heart involvement.

Today, we too can easily fall into the same trap. We can get caught up in doing all of the right things and completely miss the point of all of it: relationship with God. It is all too easy for us to become complacent through simply doing the same things repeatedly. The Lord is not so much interested in just an outward display of affection. He wants our hearts.

The Lord is not so much interested in just an outward display of affection. He wants our hearts.

I came into a saving relationship with the Lord when I was in high school. At the time I was part of a very, very traditional church. From week to week the Sunday morning services were always exactly the same. The songs changed and the pastor's message changed, but that was all. The order of service was always the same.

A few years later I married, and my wife and I moved to another state for me to attend seminary. We became a part of a church where things were very different from week to week. About a year later we made a trip home to visit family and friends. While there, we went to the church we had previously attended. I can honestly tell you that it was the most profound time of worship I had ever experienced in that church.

It should be understood that nothing at the church had changed. The order of service was exactly the same. What had changed was in me. It was not the same thing that I had experienced the previous fifty-two Sundays. For me it was new. It was fresh. Because of this I could more readily put my heart into it.

Any action, regardless of how much life there was in it the first time we did it, can become empty and meaningless if we repeat it too often. (It should be understood that good habits and discipline can be extremely beneficial in many areas of life. However, in the context of our relationship to Him, God is obviously far more interested in our hearts than just our actions alone.) Again, because we are such creatures of habit, repeating the same thing over and over will almost automatically cause it to lose its meaning and life.

So what do we do? First, simply realizing this truth will go a long way toward us overcoming this obstacle in our relationship with the Lord. Recognizing that we are indeed creatures of habit that can easily fall into a going-through-the-motions attitude is a major step in the right direction.

> ...because we are such creatures of habit, repeating the same thing over and over will almost automatically cause it to lose its meaning and life.

Beyond this, it is helpful for us to realize that, more than we desire relationship with God, He desires for us to have that relationship. In other words, the Lord does not want our relationship with Him to become boring or "old hat." If we sense that we are simply reciting words or doing things from habit, then it's time to pray and ask the Lord for creative ideas of how to keep our relationship with Him fresh and alive. God is the Author of creativity. He has more than enough ways to keep that ongoing fellowship with Him dynamic. Don't just throw out the rituals. Instead, ask God to help you strengthen and maintain your relationship through them as well as in other ways. He will.

Personal application:

1. Which of the following Christian disciplines has lost its meaning in your life through repetition?
Prayer
Bible Study
Corporate Worship
Personal Worship
Others:

2. If God were speaking to you as He did to Israel in Isaiah 1:11-14, what would He say? Are you offering meaningless sacrifices?

3. What is at least one way you can "freshen" your heart attitude in this area of your relationship with God that has become a heartless habit? Try it this week.

Part 4

The Practical How-To's of Relationship With God

Okay, so *how* do we know God?

Let's take a look at some practical ideas. All of the ethereal "let's-know-God" concepts are of no value unless you understand the how-to's. Things like Bible study, relationships with other Christians, prayer, personal and corporate worship, and seeking the Lord are all part of the process of knowing God. Each of these is an essential part of a balanced Christian walk.

Chapter 21

*Y*ou've Gotten Away
From the Book

A few years ago I attended a conference on Christian missions. One of the keynote speakers was Brother Andrew. His book *God's Smuggler,* has over ten-million copies in print. Andrew has spent a great deal of time smuggling Bibles and various pieces of Christian literature into communist (and other closed) countries. Along with this ministry, more recently God has given him the prominence to befriend national and religious leaders worldwide. During the conference he shared an incident that had recently occurred.

He was having dinner with the head of the most zealous Muslim sect on earth. During their conversation this man looked at Andrew and asked, "Do you know what the problem is with you Christians?" Andrew confided to us that he could think of quite a number of problems, but he was very interested to hear what this man thought. The man's follow-up stunned him. "The problem with you Christians is that you've gotten away from the Book."

Andrew shared that it seemed rather ironic that the head of the single-most fanatical Muslim sect would tell us our problem is that we have gotten away from the Scriptures. The reality, according to Brother Andrew, is that he's right.

Many of us have favorite Bible passages that we can quote. Some even know lengthy sections or are well-versed in certain biblical concepts. Few of us, however, really *know* the Book.

God's Word will last forever (Isaiah 40:8; 1 Peter 1:25). Long after all the physical aspects of this world are gone, the Word of the Lord will still be around. It is not just a passing fad. It is eternal.

To truly be in right relationship with the Lord, we must have an understanding of both the content and the worth of God's revealed Word, the Bible. Well-known author and teacher J.I. Packer made an interesting observation about the Word of God:

> If I were the devil, one of my first aims would be to stop folks
> from digging into the Bible. Knowing that it is the Word of God
> teaching men to know and love and serve the God of the Word,
> I should do all I could to surround it with the spiritual equivalent
> of pits, thorn hedges and man traps, to frighten people off... At
> all costs I should want to keep them from using their minds in a
> disciplined way to get the measure of its message.[1]

It seems to me the enemy of our souls does just that! He certainly does not want us delving into honest study of the Bible. He will do anything necessary to keep us from growing in our knowledge of the Word of God. One of the best things we can do to counteract this is to convince ourselves how absolutely vital it is for us to study and know the Scriptures.

Some time ago I heard a speaker at a conference talking about the Word of God. During his message he referred to Psalm 107:20:

"He sent forth His Word and healed them." The speaker then posed the question, "Is this talking about the written Word or Jesus, the Word made flesh?" Of the few hundred people in attendance, there were those who were absolutely certain that one or the other was correct. The man said the correct answer to the question is "Yes." He went on to explain that we must understand that the two are inseparable. The Word of God is the Word of God, regardless of the form.

In John 14:6, Jesus told His followers that *He* is *the truth*. Later, in John 17:17, He is praying for His disciples. He asks the Father to: "Sanctify them by the truth; *Your Word* is *truth*" (author's emphasis). Since Jesus will soon no longer be visibly with them, it seems obvious that His prayer here is referring to the spoken/written Word of God. Both Jesus, the Word made flesh, and the spoken/written Word are truth and have power in our lives. "...for You have exalted above all things Your name and *Your Word*" (Psalm 138:2b, author's emphasis).

The written Word of God is just as life-transforming as a real, personal encounter with Jesus. Unfortunately, because it is just ink on paper we often place it on a much lower plane in our society. Oh, for the Church to have a revelation of the power and significance of the written Word of God!

The book of Nehemiah relates a fascinating account of God's people realizing the value of His written Word. The rebuilding of the wall around Jerusalem had been completed. The people had begun to return to inhabit the city. After this process happened the Scripture says: "All the people assembled as one man in the square before the Water Gate. They told Ezra the scribe to bring out the Book of the Law of Moses, which the LORD had commanded for Israel" (Nehemiah 8:1). So Ezra did, and he began to read from the Book of the Law. "He read it aloud from daybreak till noon as he faced the square before the Water Gate in the presence of the men, women and others who could understand. And all the people listened attentively to the Book of the Law" (Nehemiah 8:3). They "listened attentively" from "daybreak till noon"?! What value they placed on the Word of God.

"Ezra the scribe stood on a high wooden platform built for the occasion... Ezra opened the book. All the people could see him because he was standing above them; and as he opened it, the people all stood up. Ezra praised the LORD, the great God; and all the people lifted their hands and responded, 'Amen! Amen!' Then they bowed down and worshiped the LORD with their faces to the ground" (Nehemiah 8:4-6). How different from our normal reaction today. Public reading of Scripture today is usually met with a much less enthusiastic response than those in Ezra's time. We must begin to realize the immense value in the written Word of God.

The written Word of God is just as life-transforming as a real, personal encounter with Jesus.

After we recognize the value of the Word, it's time to personally do something with it. Bill Hull shared these thoughts:

"...when church members say, 'The pastor isn't feeding me, and that is the reason I am unhappy, not growing spiritually, and generally losing my focus as a believer,' this is usually fleshly canard...Such an attitude has led to a generation of pulpit-dependent Christians who have substituted the Sunday sermon for a personal devotional life."[2]

If we truly want to know God, then studying and really knowing His Word is not just an occasional option. However, please keep in mind that simply reading Scripture in a mechanical sort of way—to complete a certain number of chapters or pages—misses the point. We need to read, study, and know the Bible in order to seek the kind of relationship with God that *He* wants us to have with Him.

Personal application:

1. How would you and your Christian friends react to a gathering from daybreak to noon simply to hear God's Word? If your pastor announced such a meeting, do you think there would be many in attendance?

2. What is one way you can show more value to the Word of God?

3. At any Christian bookstore there are Bible study guides for a certain book or theme of the Bible. Many churches offer small Bible study groups during Sunday school or through the week. One way or another begin to study and know God's Word more fully than you are currently.

Chapter 22

Avoiding the Smorgasbord Scripture Café

How was it possible for Jesus to live and minister among the people of His day without being recognized as the Messiah? They had studied the law and the prophets. The Pharisees, who were most familiar with the Scriptures, were the very ones who sentenced Jesus to death. How was this possible? Simple. The people were focused on the passages that "fit" their experiences and present situation.

At the time of Jesus' earthly ministry, Israel was under the harsh oppression of the Roman Empire. The people were not slaves, but they were certainly not completely free either. The people knew all about the prophecies of the coming Messiah being a king and having a kingdom that would last forever. They desperately wanted to be out from under the Roman rule and have their own king. In light of their understanding of the Scriptures, they fully expected the Messiah to free them from Rome.

All too often we spend time in God's Word in order to affirm what we already believe rather than to actually learn and grow.

In fact, Jesus could have been an earthly king. At one point in His ministry, He had amassed enough popularity that He could easily have declared Himself as the new ruling monarch. But as it became more and more apparent that Jesus was not interested in an earthly kingdom, His followers dwindled. As He talked of being a servant, His popularity faded. When He spoke of dying, even one of His closest followers rebuked Him.

All of them had missed the other passages. They had skipped over the Scriptures that referred to the suffering Savior. They had somehow overlooked the references to Him being a servant and His atoning death. How could they have missed such a prevalent theme? It was because those qualities didn't fit their expectations. They wanted a king, not a servant.

Today, we as Christians desire for God's Word to be our guide. However, the culture in which we live, our upbringing, our education, our experiences, and even our personality type can color the way we think and act. These influences frequently even affect the way we read the Bible.

Too often we practice what could be referred to as cafeteria-style Christianity. We walk along the smorgasbord looking at the various choices. There are certain sections of Scripture that seem very appealing, so we choose to partake of those. Other passages, those that seem less inviting, we choose to leave behind.

All too often we spend time in God's Word in order to affirm what we already believe rather than to actually learn and grow. We are more ready to prove our present way of thinking than we are to allow God to show us *His* truth.

Recently I felt compelled to study a particular topic from a scriptural perspective. My prayer before beginning this endeavor went something like this, "Lord, I know what I already believe about this subject. Please show me the fullness of Your heart from Your Word." I was amazed that in my honest, truly-seeking-the-heart-of-the-Lord study, I saw things I had never considered before.

I remember being involved in a Bible study as a teenager, not long after I was born-again. During one session of the study, I made a statement that I thought was quite profound. "I believe the Bible is the Word of God," I said, "but it is only in its present form because God had to work through human vessels. If He could give us His Word in its purest form, it would look quite different than the way that we know it. Everything would be much more orderly, probably in specific sections under topical headings." This idea sounds practical, but now, decades after having made this statement, I am more and more convinced that God purposely gave us His Word in the form it is in. It forces us to search the Scriptures and dig for truth. Searching and digging, in turn, causes us to look at the whole of Scripture, not just one particular area.

I heard a statement quite some time ago by author and teacher Tim Hansel. The statement has stuck with me for years. "All of our theology must eventually become biography." In essence our biography is our personal history. It reflects the real us. The biography of a Christian should reflect who God is and what He has been, is, and will be in our lives. Unfortunately, most Christians today prefer to fit their theology to their biography. If a particular passage does not fit into our preconceived ideas, then it is usually ignored.

Long ago Augustine said, "If you believe in the gospel what you like, and reject what you don't like, it is not the gospel you believe, but yourself."

What we need is an openness to the Holy Spirit to illuminate the Word that it might impact our lives in the way *He* wants it to. We need to endeavor to set aside our cultural biases and see what it really says.

I have often seen people justify their actions because they found a particular passage of Scripture to support what they were doing.

Simply quoting a few choice scriptures and ignoring the rest of the
Bible's counsel on the topic does not make it right. The devil even
did that (Matthew 4:1-11; Luke 4:1-13). The Bible can be a lamp to
our feet and a light to our path (Psalm 119:105), but only as much
as we will allow it to be. We must seek the whole truth on every
issue.

Not long ago I was driving on a rather congested roadway. For
some reason my attention was drawn to the driver of the car in front
of me. Every time he used his rearview mirror, he stretched his neck
and lifted himself a bit to see into it. I thought it seemed very pecu-
liar that he did not adjust the mirror. Instead he adjusted himself
every time he used the mirror. Although this idea is very awkward
for driving, we need to learn to do that very thing with our use of the
Bible. Instead of adjusting the Bible to fit our situations, we need to
adjust our lives to fit what Scripture teaches.

Personal application:

*1. Hypothetically speaking, do you think that people today would be any bet-
ter at recognizing Jesus as our Messiah if He came today?*

*2. What is a theological opinion you feel strongly about and even judge oth-
ers for when they don't, in your opinion, believe the correct way? Have you
studied the whole Scriptures to get God's perspective on the subject? If not,
why not try it?*

*3. Is there an answer you are waiting for God to reveal to you that you might
be missing because you haven't "dug" for an answer in His Word? (Are you
missing the Messiah, so to speak, because you're only looking for what you
want to see?) If so, make the question very specific and then do some thorough
research from the Bible.*

Chapter 23

Getting the
Most Out
of the Bible

*T*hroughout the centuries biblical scholars have agreed that there are certain rules or guidelines we must follow in order to arrive at a proper understanding of the Bible. Without considering these points it is easy to misinterpret Scripture. Without some type of rules to govern our interpretation, we become masters over Scripture instead of students of the Word.

This concept is far too broad in scope for this brief section of a small book like this, but here are a few simple, practical principles of proper Bible interpretation:

• What was the common meaning of the word(s) being used?

I wish I were making this story up, but I'm not. It's true. A friend of mine once heard a radio preacher talking about the woman who was closest to Jesus. It wasn't Mary or Martha or any of the other women we might commonly associate with Jesus' ministry. This man was talking about a different woman. Her name was Verily (pronounced va-ri´-lee). Jesus talked to her often: "Verily, verily I say unto thee..." Obviously this is a rather extreme illustration, but the point is still the same. A modern language translation of the Bible (like the New International Version or the New King James) can really help with this area. Translations like these help capture the meaning of words and phrases in a language that we can understand today.

In referring to the Bible, I once heard someone comment, "Don't tell me what you think it says, or even what you'd like to believe it says, just tell me what it says. If God had meant to say something else, He would have done it. He said what He meant." That is very solid advice.

• What do other clear passages say about the same subject?

Too often an opinion that clearly violates other Scriptures is put forth based on one particular passage. Second Peter 3:16 tells us that some things in the Bible are more difficult to understand than others. The clear passages of Scripture must therefore help interpret the difficult verses.

Allow me to illustrate this concept. Next summer, if you were to read a newspaper headline that said, "Total Eclipse Tomorrow at 7:15," you would have no way of knowing for certain whether it would be 7:15A.M. or P.M. However, if the article mentioned that the eclipse would enhance what already promised to be a spectacular sunset, you would know it was obviously 7:15P.M. The clearer section helped interpret the more obscure reference. The same principle holds true in Bible interpretation. It is not acceptable to violate clear passages based on those that are more difficult to understand.

- **What other historical facts have bearing on the meaning?**

What is the setting of the writing? Who was the writer (their position and background)? To whom was the writing addressed? What was the purpose of the writing? Is the historical time frame of the writing significant, etc.?

For example, when reading the gospel accounts of Jesus' earthly ministry, it can be very helpful to be aware that the book of Matthew was written primarily for a Jewish audience, and the book of Mark seems to be more geared to Gentiles. This helps explain some of the phrases and words that are used in these concurrent, yet different, biographies of Jesus' life. A good study Bible and quality reference materials can help supply important historical information.

- **What is the context of the passage?**

This one is the easiest for the non-biblical scholar to understand and use, but is also the one that is violated most frequently. Let me explain.

One of my favorite quotes on this subject is, "A text out of its context is a pretext." Nearly any statement outside of the context in which it was made can be misunderstood. Have you ever been quoted out of context? It is easy to take the words of another person and use them completely out of context. However, the results can sometimes be devastating. This can be true with God's Word also.

In the first verse of Matthew 6, Jesus said, "Be careful not to do your acts of righteousness before men..." In the context of what He was saying, Jesus was talking about doing those acts of righteousness to be seen by men. If your motivation is to impress the people, then, in God's sight, those acts are worthless.

However, that statement, taken strictly at face value, would be impossible for me. I regularly teach in front of hundreds of people. I do "acts of righteousness before men" on a regular basis. In the words quoted above, I must be wrong. That's because those words are taken out of the original context.

It has been said that you can prove anything from the Bible. That may be a bit overstated, but certainly many things, if taken out of context, can be "proven." If we are really to mature in the Lord, then we must realize that a proper understanding of Scripture must occur within its context. We cannot simply take a passage out of its original setting in order to make it fit our personal ideas.

- **What is the application of the passage intended to be?**

I once read a magazine article that illustrates this point. The author used the story of Joash (2 Kings 11:1-21; 2 Chronicles 22:10-23:21) as his basis. Joash, a mere infant and the only remaining heir to the throne of Judah, was forced into hiding for six years because of his evil aunt Athaliah. Based on this factual story, the author went on to make the assertion that every spiritually healthy person absolutely *must* serve a term of hiddenness. Although this sounds like a fine principle, it cannot be stated emphatically from Scripture and most assuredly not from this section of Scripture.

Please understand that this statement has merit. I have frequently seen that those whom God has chosen to use in a mighty way have spent much time "hidden," apparently in preparation for God's use. However, to state this principle as an absolute, especially based strictly on this story, goes beyond the obvious intention of the passage.

It may be acceptable, upon observing an ongoing theme in historical passages throughout the Scriptures, to derive a conclusion based on a broad spectrum of experiences. However, taking a historical account from Scripture and, based on a one-time historical occurrence, creating an all-encompassing truth is definitely not preserving the context of the passage.

Unfortunately, this type of teaching is popular, even trendy, in the Church today: a biblical account is shared and application is made far beyond what Scripture actually says. The reality is that there are plenty of clearly stated scriptural principles that we the Church are not doing. We certainly do not need someone's opinion (stated as fact) that may or may not be correct.

The deceptiveness of this type of teaching is that what applications are made from any given story are completely at the whim of the one teaching. For example, why did this particular author not share about Joash being hidden in the temple for *six years* (2 Kings 11:3; 2 Chronicles 22:12) and assert, then, that we must all be hidden for six years? I could share other similar ideas from the same story, but I think the point is clear.

The usual answer I hear when I have confronted this type of teaching is that the truly spiritual man can discern truth. Please forgive my skepticism, but I have seen too many "spiritual" men deceived. I have even seen two gifted teachers using the same text and drawing contradictory conclusions.

The reality is that we must be very careful with how we interpret the Bible. We must do honest, prayerful digging and searching to find the whole truth. We cannot simply take a single thought or idea and run with it. We must look at the whole of Scripture and check it out thoroughly. Our aim should be 2 Timothy 2:15: "Do your best to present yourself to God as one approved, a workman who does not need to be ashamed and who correctly handles the Word of truth." (See also 2 Timothy 3:16-17.)

We have often come to the conclusion that unless some idea is brand new, then it is not of any value. We have forgotten that generations of people who had a vital, personal relationship with the living God came before us.

Unfortunately, today there are many Christians who have been affected in some way by poor understanding and poor teaching of the Word of God. Please realize that we certainly have not abandoned the Bible. What we have lost, in many cases, is the understanding of how to interpret Scripture correctly. A proper grasp of God's Word can only come if we have a correct understanding of how to interpret God's Word.

Too often we have left behind centuries of biblical study and research. The writings and revelations of our forefathers often lie untouched in dusty books on even dustier shelves. We have often come to the conclusion that unless some idea is brand new, then it is not of any value. We have forgotten that generations of people who had a vital, personal relationship with the living God came before us. And today we have the nerve to think that we are the first generation to really walk in the fullness of the truth of God's Word. How arrogant and foolish!

The Bible is 66 books, written by 39 men, in three languages on three continents over a period of 1,500 years, yet it has uncanny consistency. In order to really understand it, we need to follow certain principles like those mentioned here.

The people of the church at Berea were lauded for their diligence at searching the Scriptures (Acts 17:11). We too must become adept at our handling of God's Word.

Personal application:

1. If you don't have a good grasp of these principles to aid in accurate study of God's Word, why not copy the highlighted questions to a 3"x5" card and tuck it in your Bible as a reminder?

2. Which of these principles are you most likely to ignore? Next time you study a passage or a topic, concentrate on diligently applying this particular principle.

3. If you've never read from a Bible commentary or used a study Bible, check one out from your church library or purchase one at your local Christian bookstore to aid your study of God's Word.

Chapter 24

God Said It.
That Settles It.

There are ministers today teaching that God teaches us through our spirit, not through our mind. This seemingly rampant teaching is very misguided and is one major hindrance I have encountered to proper Bible interpretation.

Among the many passages of Scripture that are in direct opposition to this teaching is 2 Timothy 2:15: "Do your best to present yourself to God as one approved, a workman who does not need to be ashamed and who correctly handles the word of truth." The Greek word that is translated here as "do your best" literally means to "make an effort." The KJV renders this word as "study." If we are going to do our best at handling the word of truth, then clearly it has the connotation of using our mind to think and ponder and study.

First Chronicles 28:12 says this: "He (God) gave him (David) the plans of all that the Spirit had put in his *mind* for the courts of the temple of the LORD and all the surrounding rooms, for the treasuries of the temple of God and for the treasuries for the dedicated things" (author's emphasis). Likewise, God will speak to our minds today through His written Word.

Paul tells Timothy, "Reflect on what I am saying, for the Lord will give you insight into all this" (2 Timothy 2:7). The Greek words in this passage clearly have to do with the thought process of rational thinking. Paul even tells us that it is possible (and wrong) to have a great deal of zeal with no knowledge (Romans 10:2).

In his book *A Godward Life*, John Piper shares about this idea in a chapter called "Think Deeply Clearly." Piper plays the part of Paul, the apostle, and shares these thoughts:

> ...even in raising the objection against thinking, you are thinking! You cannot escape the necessity of thinking. God's call is to do it well...Thinking and asking questions are the only ways you will ever understand what I want to communicate in my letters. Either you will do it poorly, or you will do it well. So do not be a child in your thinking. Be a babe in evil, but in thinking be mature (1 Corinthians 14:20, RSV). As the Master said, "wise as serpents and innocent as doves" (Matthew 10:16, RSV).[1]

Perhaps the most devastating part of the anti-mind teaching is that, if followed to its logical conclusion, we become supreme over Scripture. In referring to any given Bible passage, many times I have heard someone say, "God will quicken it (make it alive) to your spirit." The obvious ending point, then, is that if we do not receive some sort of internal "knowing," we need not believe it or obey it.

Recently the absurdity of this teaching was made clear to me in a new way. A couple had come to my pastor saying they wanted to get married. They had been attending our church for several months and decided they would like to be married there. One slight obstacle arose in the counseling sessions: he was in the process of a divorce from his present wife, a divorce that he had been planning for several years. My pastor pointed out to the man the very clear scriptural teaching regarding divorce. His response was, "I know the Bible says that, but God will have to speak it to my spirit for me to stop what I'm doing."

Either we believe the Book is God's Word or we do not. There is no middle ground.

Some time ago a woman who had been very divisive in a particular church was confronted on the issue. She was shown very clear Scripture passages that addressed divisiveness. At the end she made this statement, "God is going to have to show it to me before I will believe

Perhaps the most devastating part of the anti-mind teaching is that, if followed to its logical conclusion, we become supreme over Scripture.

it." Wrong! If it is in the Bible, then God *has* already made it perfectly clear. The Scripture is the Word of God. It is given to us to be believed and obeyed.

There is a bumper sticker I have seen that says, "God said it. I believe it. That settles it." In reality we should change that kind of thinking. Our heart attitude should be, "God said it. That settles it." As mentioned earlier, we need to line up our thinking with His Word, not His Word with our thinking.

One important point that is crucial for all of us is this: we must always maintain a humble, teachable attitude. I know a man who is a highly respected teacher in the Body of Christ. He is a very scholarly man. He understands both Greek and Hebrew and has spent many years studying the Scriptures. Over the years I have seen him powerfully teach truth from God's Word. I have also heard him give his opinions on certain topics, even on Bible passages, but always he emphasizes that these are opinions. He is careful to separate that which is very plain in the Word of God from that which is not. I refer to this as doctrinal humility.

Most of us today are sorely lacking in this area. We are certain that the things we believe are more correct than the ideas of others.

I once heard a man make a statement that was very profound. He said that we believe most strongly the stance that we heard first.

Once we have taken that stance as our own, it will take a great measure of reason and evidence to move us away from our belief.

Let me illustrate this. John Average-Christian is in his early twenties. John believes he is called to pastor and heads off to a particular seminary. After the prescribed amount of time, John graduates and his doctrinal beliefs are very much in line with the teaching of that particular seminary. If you were to ask John why he believes the way he does, he would not necessarily say that it was because of what he was taught. Instead, he would tell you very plainly that it is because he is following the clear teaching of Scripture.

For the sake of argument, let's rewind this scenario. We'll use the same John Average-Christian who is called to pastor. However, this time he will go to a very different seminary. The doctrinal beliefs on issues such as end-times and predestination are radically different than the first seminary. In this scenario, John will again go through the necessary time and graduate. His belief system is very different than in the first scenario. Once again, if you were to ask him why he believes the way he does, he would again tell you that he is following the clear teaching of the Bible.

Obviously we cannot recreate this example in real life. It is impossible to rewind someone's life, erase their memory banks, and start over. However, this same scenario is played out day after day all over the world. Seminaries and Bible colleges with very different views are consistently turning out students who believe just as they have been instructed.

Please understand that there is nothing wrong with teaching or even with believing what we have been taught. However, all of these varying viewpoints cannot be correct in their interpretation of Scripture. For years brilliant scholars have arrived at very different conclusions about certain areas of doctrine. For any one of us to assert that any belief but our own shows idiocy would be the height of arrogance and pride. That's why we need doctrinal humility. We must be willing to dialogue and discuss and keep an open mind.

One final point to conclude this section: we must realize that although purity in our doctrine is important, it is not the *most* important thing. Jesus did not say that people would know we were His disciples because we all agree on every point of doctrine. He said, "By this all men will know that you are My disciples, if you *love one another"* (John 13:35, author's emphasis). The A Paul said it this way, "If I can...fathom all mysteries and all knowledge... but have not love, I am nothing (1 Corinthians 13:2).

Our beliefs must be based solidly on the Bible, yet at the same time we should maintain a humble, teachable position, recognizing that none of us have a lock on all truth.

Personal application:

1. What's the difference between "God said it. I believe it. That settles it." and "God said it. That settles it."? Is there something you've been waiting to believe (or perhaps refusing to believe) that should be settled already?

2. Pick one of your personally held doctrinal beliefs and research (thoroughly and honestly) another perspective.

3. Is there someone whose difference in doctrinal belief has prevented you from loving them as a brother or sister in Christ? Pray that God will grant you the ability and grace to love them anyway.

$\mathcal{T}$he Virtual Reality Church

$\mathcal{M}$y pastor and I both have overactive imaginations. Quite some time ago we were discussing the possibility of someone creating a virtual reality church. The building, the decor, the pastor, the worship leader, singers, instrumentalists, choir, even the congregational members could all be stored on a CD-ROM disk for a computer. Then you could make your own decisions every time you decide to "go" to church. Your personal preferences would dictate the style of architecture and surroundings. You could choose a pastor (or several); virtually any pastor in the world could be accessible. You would be able to pick your own worship leader. The instruments being played, the harmonies being sung, the style(s) of music, even the songs used would all be your choice. You would even get to determine who you would like to have at church that day. You could pick the people you really like, or, more importantly, leave out the ones you dislike.

The beauty of this whole concept is that *you* get to make all of the decisions, and no one else can mess things up for you. No worries about whether the message for the day might be too close to home for your comfort; you choose the topic and even the style of delivery. You would never need to sing songs with which you are unfamiliar or uncomfortable; you pick the songs. Even the volume of the music is yours to control; make it as loud or as quiet as you want. Best of all, you never have to be concerned about relating to people who make you uneasy. No bothersome relationships in the virtual reality church—only the folks you can really understand and relate to.

The whole concept is so perfect I am thinking about patenting it—if for no other reason than to keep anyone from actually doing it. You see, relationships with brothers and sisters in Christ are a big part of the Kingdom of God. A church without people is not a church. We need one another.

From the very beginning of time relationships with others have been a part of God's plan for mankind. In Genesis 2:18 God said, "It is not good for the man to be alone..." Have you ever wondered why it was "not good"? Was God concerned that Adam might be attacked by a roving street gang? Perhaps the Lord thought he might be devoured by a man-eating lion? Of course not. This was prior to the first sin. Before the fall, before sin, the Lord declared that man's solitude was not good because it was contrary to God's plan. Right from the beginning relationships were part of His design.

Unfortunately, throughout history mankind has demonstrated that we do not understand the importance of relationships. This is more true today than ever before. We are driven by a desire for achievement and accomplishment. Our jobs, educational goals, athletic endeavors, and many other things frequently take precedence over our relationships. We are far more interested in what we can achieve than in simply forming relationships.

Scripture is very clear about the importance of relationships among God's people. "How good and pleasant it is when brothers live together in unity... For there the Lord bestows His blessing, even life forevermore" (Psalm 133:1-3). "Be devoted to one another in brotherly love. Honor one another above yourselves" (Romans 12:10). "Above all, love each other deeply..." (1 Peter 4:8). These passages and many others point out the absolute necessity of strong, caring, loving relationships.

> **"Part of the measuring rod of how you're doing in your relationship with God is how you're dong in your relationship with your brothers and sisters in Christ."**

Several years ago my pastor made a powerful statement that has stuck with me. "Part of the measuring rod of how you're doing in your relationship with God is how you're doing in your relationship with your brothers and sisters in Christ." It's true. The two cannot be separated.

In the ninth chapter of Acts, Saul of Tarsus was traveling to Damascus to imprison the followers of Jesus. On the way, Jesus spoke to Saul.

> As he neared Damascus on his journey, suddenly a light from heaven flashed around him. He fell to the ground and heard a voice say to him, "Saul, Saul, why do you persecute Me?"
>
> "Who are You, Lord?" Saul asked.
>
> "I am Jesus, Whom you are persecuting," He replied (Acts 9:3-5).

I find it interesting that Saul was not rebuked for persecuting *the Church*. Instead, Jesus clearly says that Saul was persecuting *Him*. This encounter must have had quite an impact on Saul's (later to become Paul) theology. Several times in his later writings he refers to the Church as "the Body of Christ." Paul realized that the Lord has so completely tied us as believers to Himself that we have somehow become a part of who He is. Consequently, our relationships with one another will ultimately affect our relationship with Him.

Jesus obviously had this concept in mind when He said: "But if you do not forgive men their sins, your heavenly Father will not forgive your sins" (Matthew 6:15). Not being in proper relationship with one another can ultimately sever our relationship with God.

We cannot have a relationship with God in a vacuum, apart from the rest of the Body of Christ. We must not have the attitude of, "I can make it with Jesus. I don't need anyone else." Jesus made this concept very clear when He stated: "...whatever you did for one of the least of these brothers of Mine, you did for Me" (Matthew 25:40). Our relationships with one another will affect our relationship with God.

For us as Christians the very essence of the Christian life is found in relationship. "For anyone who does not love his brother, whom he has seen, cannot love God, whom he has not seen" (1 John 4:20b). Please note that this passage does not say that if you don't love your brother you *might not* be able to love God. It says you *cannot*. Part of the demonstration of how much we love God is how much we love our fellow believers. Our relationship with one another reflects our relationship with God.

Personal application:

1. If you could create your own Virtual Church, who would you leave out? Perhaps God has some work to do in your heart toward those fellow believers.

2. Have you seen, prior to this time, how intrinsically God has tied Himself to His people? If not, ask the Lord to grant you a more complete understanding of the Body of Christ.

3. Today make a tangible effort to demonstrate your love for God by demonstrating your love for His people. Consider a very special act of kindness for one of your Christian friends or even a believer you don't know.

orship—
A Way of Life

A couple of years ago I heard a minister share about visiting another church with a friend. As they walked to their car after the service that Sunday morning, the friend confided, "I really enjoyed the pastor's message, but I didn't get much out of the worship." The minister looked at him and asked, "Have you ever considered what difference that makes?"

The point of his question was simple. In essence he was asking, "Who is our worship for?" It is not ultimately so we can receive something (although that may indeed happen during times of worship). Our acts of praise and worship are for God. Whether or not we "get anything out of it" is immaterial. We worship because He is worthy.

When we honestly have that kind of attitude, then neither circumstances nor feelings nor emotions can deter us from honoring our Sovereign Lord. Regardless of any external or internal storms we may encounter, we can still worship God because He is always worthy. In the true act of worship we are less interested in what we can get and more concerned about what we can give.

In the true act of worship we are less interested in what we can get and more concerned about what we can give.

Several years ago I heard a man speaking about the importance of the Word of God. During his teaching he shared this passage: "Seven times a day I praise You for Your righteous laws" (Psalm 119:164). His point from this verse is that we need to praise God for His Word. As I listened, my thought process went something like this: "Yes, that's right. However, do we praise God seven times a day for anything? And if we did, would it make a difference in our lives?"

As I mentioned earlier, I have a very vivid imagination. Consequently, in thinking about this praising-God-seven-times-a-day passage, I began to wonder how we could make this reality. Perhaps we could do it like this:

1. First thing in the morning
2. Right after breakfast
3. Midmorning
4. Right after lunch
5. Midafternoon
6. Right after supper
7. Before bedtime

What do you suppose would happen if we actually stopped for just a few minutes at each one of those times and gave thanks and praise to God? I'm not even referring to just thanking Him for His Word. You can pick the topic. Just praise Him.

Praising God seven times each day does not need to become a liturgy for our daily lives. To me it is more of an attitude. We who have been brought out of darkness into His marvelous light should be the most thankful, most praising people on earth. It is not essential that we count out seven separate times each day and honor the Lord. However, sometimes it becomes necessary for us to do something really radical to shake ourselves in our relationship with Him. Let me put it this way: do you think that if you did that every day it would make a difference in your life? Of course it would.

Some time ago I shared this concept at a large church where I was ministering. This particular church had a pastor on their staff whose main job was to increase the awareness of missions within their church and to oversee mission outreaches from their church. This man came to me after the service and told me something I will never forget. He said this, "That seven-times-a-day idea is really interesting. We look at the Muslims and we think they're really fanatical because five times a day they bow down toward Mecca and pray. Do you know why they do that?" I assured him I had no idea. "It's because when Mohammed started the Muslim religion it was the practice of the Christians to pray seven times each day. He decided that was too fanatical and settled on only five times a day." I was stunned.

I believe that the Lord is looking for some fanatics today! He's looking for people who will pursue Him at all costs.

Luke records the story of the woman who broke the very expensive alabaster jar of perfume and poured it on Jesus (Luke 7:36-50). The Pharisees were aghast that He would allow such a sinful woman to touch Him. Jesus simply told them a story about forgiveness and love and then asked them a question. He then equated her costly sacrifice, including the jar of perfume, her time and her affection, with her love for Him.

The reality is that to Jesus she was demonstrating true worship. She seemingly had no thought of receiving from this act. It was simply an act of honoring the One she adored. From Jesus' reaction, it would appear that her worship was exactly right.

In discussing this concept, it is vital to realize that true worship is ultimately not just an occasional action on our part. It must permeate our entire life. Again, it must be an attitude of the heart.

I find it interesting that one of the most often quoted worship passages is frequently misunderstood. John 4:23 tells us that God is seeking "worshipers." "Yet a time is coming and has now come when the true worshipers will worship the Father in spirit and truth, *for they are the kind of worshipers the Father seeks*" (John 4:23, author's emphasis). It does not say that He is looking for "worship." Instead of using the word that refers to the action, Jesus used the word referring to the person. A worshiper does not just offer an occasional sacrifice of praise through song. A true worshiper lives a life of worship in all that he or she says and does through a consistent focus on God.

Personal application:

1. Do you go to church primarily to get from God or to give—honor, praise, love, adoration, worship—to Him?

2. Do you take time to simply praise and worship God with no thought of receiving? Do you honor Him in word, thought, and deed? Make the choice that regardless of whether you feel any excitement or receive any tangible benefits from it, you will worship God. He is always worthy.

3. For today (or tomorrow if it's late in the day now), do praise God seven times. At the end of the day, evaluate if it made a difference in your day.

Chapter 27

Prayer— Just Do It!

*A*nother practical part of our relationship with God is prayer. The Bible devotes a large amount of space to the topic of prayer. It appears to be something that the Lord greatly values.

However, we often view prayer as a mystery. We are frequently uncertain about the proper way to pray. We question our words, our thoughts, our faith. We even sometimes wonder (privately, of course) whether there is really any use in praying.

The second half of James 5:16 says: "The prayer of a righteous man is powerful and effective." One day the reality of this verse dawned on me. In and of myself I am most certainly not righteous. However, because of Jesus' death and resurrection, I have been made righteous. Therefore this verse is talking about me. It says that my prayer is "powerful and effective." It doesn't say that I must learn to pray in a powerful or effective manner. It simply states that my prayer is powerful and effective.

This verse is only for Christians, but it is for every Christian. There is no one righteous (Romans 3:10) apart from the blood of Jesus. However, those who have been cleansed by that precious blood have been made righteous. Therefore, this verse is applicable to any Christian. When you, as a believer in the atoning work of the cross, pray, your prayer is powerful and effective. That's a promise from God's Word to you..

It seems to me that people are frequently looking for someone to teach them exactly how to pray. They want a formula. A carefully planned outline of the right steps for prayer would make them really happy. This idea is not new.

One day, after observing Jesus praying, one of His disciples said, "Lord, teach us to pray..." (Luke 11:1). Jesus' response was to share with them what we refer to as The Lord's Prayer. In looking at the whole of Scripture, it seems obvious that Jesus' intent was not so much just to give them the exact words to pray but to impart the heart intent of prayer as a whole.

The example He gave them is very potent. It contains elements of worship ("hallowed be Your Name") as well as petitions for God's kingdom to be established ("Your kingdom come") and His plans and purposes to be accomplished ("Your will be done"). There is a request for provision of material needs ("give us today our daily bread"), a plea for forgiveness ("forgive us our sins"), and an entreaty to be kept from further sin ("lead us not into temptation").

To me, one of the most amazing aspects about this prayer is its brevity. It is extremely dynamic yet very concise. Luke's version (Luke 11:2-4) contains just 34 words. The lengthier edition (Matthew 6:9-13) is made up of 52 words. Many Christians often say more than that just praying before a meal!

The truth is that God is not impressed with people's ability to keep praying on and on. In fact, Jesus seems to indicate that the opposite might be better. Just before He shared the above prayer with His disciples, He said this: "And when you pray, do not keep on babbling like pagans, for they think they will be heard because of their many words" (Matthew 6:7). Jesus not only told them not to be long-winded in prayer, He then went on and demonstrated how to avoid it.

My personal opinion is that God may prefer frequent shorter prayers. I certainly cannot cite chapter and verse for that, but it seems obvious that the greater the frequency throughout the day (instead of relegating it to only a certain "prayer time"), the more prayer has become a part of us.

The truth is that God is not impressed with people's ability to keep praying on and on.

Please realize that there is nothing inherently wrong with praying for a long time. There were times when Jesus was certainly not at a loss for words in prayer. The entire seventeenth chapter of John is a prayer of Jesus. In the garden of Gethsemane, Jesus apparently prayed for more than an hour (Mark 14:37). There seems to be nothing wrong with lengthy praying. However, there is obviously no correlation between the number of words and the acceptableness of the prayer to God. He is always far more interested in the heart than in how long the prayer takes.

I also find it interesting to note that neither the time nor the location of the prayer seems to be extremely important. Jesus prayed in the morning (Mark 1:35), but He also prayed at night (Luke 6:12). He prayed outdoors and indoors. Jesus frequently prayed alone (Mark 1:35; 6:46; Luke 5:16; 6:12), but He sometimes prayed in groups (John 17) or even in crowds (Matthew 14:19; John 11:41-42).

Perhaps you are familiar with international evangelist Reinhard Bonnke. Hundreds of thousands of souls have come into the kingdom of God through his ministry. Bonnke credits a great measure of the success he has had to the people who consistently pray for him. A few years ago I heard the woman who leads the intercession team for Bonnke. Please understand that this is her job. She spends hours a day praying. As she spoke she made one simple statement that has stuck with me ever since. She said, "It is not how long you pray or how 'powerfully' you pray—it is *that* you pray that counts."

Bob Sorge said it like this, "There isn't a right way or a wrong way to cry out to God. Just cry! You need no tips or guidelines, just cry from the depths of your heart to Him. He hears His children."[1] In saying this Sorge echoes the words of David from Psalm 34:15:

There is obviously no correlation between the number of words and the acceptableness of the prayer to God. He is always far more interested in the heart than in how long the prayer takes.

"The eyes of the LORD are on the righteous and His ears are attentive to their cry."

During His earthly ministry, Jesus demonstrated the priority of prayer. Luke 5:16 tells us: "But Jesus often withdrew to lonely places and prayed." The fact that the holy Son of God found it necessary to pray "often" should tell us something.

When Jesus drew apart for prayer, it was definitely a time to talk to the Father, but also important was the aspect of listening; it was a time for Him to hear from His Father. Obviously Jesus had a very clear understanding of what His purpose was. However, it seems apparent that it was during these times alone with God that the plan was reinforced and more details were understood. We also need to listen as we pray, not just talk.

A word of caution is probably in order here. There are some well-meaning Christians who insist that a certain amount of time should be spent in prayer daily. Some say at least one hour per day (based on Jesus' words in Mark 14:37-38: "...Could you not keep watch for one hour? Watch and pray..."). Others prefer two hours and 24 minutes (2.4 hours = the tithe from a 24-hour day). The truth is that the Bible does not give us a specific time allotment for daily prayer. If you are currently not even praying for five minutes a day, an hour is not a realistic starting point. Start where and when you are able and learn the discipline as well as the privilege of prayer.

I once heard the wife of a pastor make a startling statement. She said, "I knew I was in trouble when I reached the point that I would rather shop than pray." Prayer can be fun, but it's not always. Sometimes it is just plain work. (Hmmm...sounds like much of the rest of life.) But it is worth the effort.

Prayer can and should be a vital part of our relationship with the Lord. It is the essential link through which we can pour out our hearts to Him. It is a time when He speaks to us. It is a dialogue with Him and, as such, a vital part of our relationship with Him.

Personal application:

1. As a Christian, does it change anything for you to understand that your prayers are powerful and effective? How so?

2. Who is someone who you always admire when they pray publicly? Are you intimidated because you aren't so eloquent? Does it help to know that praying what is in your heart is what God wants to hear from you?

3. Is prayer a priority in your life? Or could you say with the pastor's wife, "I know I'm in trouble because I'd rather _____ than pray"? What should you do to remedy this situation?

Chapter 29

Practicing the Presence of God

Throughout this book I have alluded to the idea of a relationship with God that permeates our whole life every day. Although I have sporadically mentioned the concept several times, this book would be incomplete if I did not offer a bit more depth on this idea. After all, if the Lord is always with us in all we do wherever we are, it seems inappropriate to suggest that we should relegate our relationship with Him to just a few brief moments each day. Please recognize that structured times of prayer, worship, and Bible study are essential to our growth as Christians. They will give us the undergirding we need for a solid ongoing relationship. However, an honest relationship with God must consist of more than just those things.

In his book *A Diary of Private Prayer*, John Baillie shared this prayer: "Yet let me not, when this morning prayer is said, think my worship ended and spend the day in forgetfulness of Thee. Rather from these moments of quietness let light go forth, and joy, and power, that will remain with me through all hours of the day."[1] The discipline of the more structured times offer us a framework for the fullness of our relationship with the Lord.

> **If our relationship with an omnipresent God is to be honest, then that relationship must include all we do.**

Cultivating an awareness of God in our daily lives is vital. As we recognize His presence in us and with us, then relationship with Him throughout the day is a natural occurrence. A medieval monk, Brother Lawrence, talked of practicing the presence of God. He recognized that God was with Him in all he did and consequently used all he did to nurture his relationship with the Lord. His prayer was:

> My God, since You are with me, and since it is Your will that I should apply my mind to these outward things, I pray that You will give me the grace to remain with You and keep company with You. But so that my work may be better, Lord, work with me; receive my work and possess all my affections.[2]

If our relationship with an omnipresent God is to be honest, then that relationship must, as Brother Lawrence suggested, include all we do. In her extremely practical book *Enjoying the Presence of God*, Jan Johnson said it this way:

> It seems unusual, maybe even funny, to consider God's presence in the parts of our lives that are not necessarily intellectual pursuits—dreaming, eating, playing sports. Paying attention to God's presence is wider and deeper than thinking about God all the time. It involves the ordinary activities of our entire being—feeling, sensing, listening and moving in such a way that watering

plants, playing volleyball, and walking on the beach take on a rhythm of prayer.[3]

Eighteenth-century Jesuit priest Jean Nicholas phrased it like this: "We are not incessantly making vocal prayers, but our heart is turned toward God, always listening for the voice of God, always ready to do His holy will."

The more we grow in our understanding of God through His Word as well as through structured times of prayer and worship, the more natural our everyday relationship with Him becomes. It is the outflow of a wellspring of a life turned toward God.

However, this is not to say that advancing our relationship with God in the everyday activities of life will always be easy. Some tasks seem naturally to cause frustration. Other activities can bring us anxiety or fear. In these times we may need to make a conscious effort to develop our relationship with the Lord. Jan Johnson shared these thoughts:

> I could only find eleven business telephone bills for the year—where was the twelfth? I could save a considerable amount in taxes if only I could find that bill! I'm careful with my paperwork for my business, but every year I seem to lose one thing—okay, two or three things.
>
> I prayed, *I know, God, I'm getting upset. This isn't a crisis.*
>
> I've looked in last year's files—I've looked in this year's files. The bill vanished. In what miserable, obscure place could I have put it?
>
> *Yes, God, I'm beating up on myself. I know this is wrong. Help me stop.*
>
> Back and forth I battle with myself when I figure our income tax. I go from the despair of losing documents to the ecstasy of saving a few dollars. At the end of the day, I'm exhausted. A few years ago, I realized something else as well. I missed God that day. Sure, I bellowed out a breath prayer now and then, but I missed God's abiding presence, something I'd learned to enjoy.
>
> That was when I noticed the candle in the middle of the dining room table where I worked. I resolved that the next year I would light that candle to remind me to recall God's presence as I work.

And so it's been the last few years. Throughout the roller-coaster emotions of that day, I see in my peripheral vision that candle burning and I mumble, "yes" and "thank You" (that I have an income). The day doesn't sail by smoothly, but that's not the point. I don't keep company with God to guarantee myself a happy life. I do it because I need God, because "I want to know Christ and the power of His resurrection" (Philippians 3:10). Even on such a day, I can enjoy God's presence. I walk through self-flagellation and self-exaltation with a little more grace.[4]

Making the conscious effort of lighting the candle helped Jan Johnson to broaden her understanding of God's presence even in the midst of a less-than-enjoyable experience. There was nothing special or "magical" in the candle or even the lighting of it. However, it caused her to focus on the reality of God a bit more. Sometimes we, too, need to take steps with deliberate forethought to help us grow in our relationship with the Lord.

> **The more we are aware of God's abiding presence in our lives, the more we begin to readily recognize His hand at work.**

This entire concept of recognizing God's presence in our lives and interacting with Him throughout the day seems to be somewhat self-perpetuating. The more we are aware of God's abiding presence in our lives, the more we begin to readily recognize His hand at work.

Holy coincidences occur. Scripture we skipped over yesterday seems to shout our names today. Information suddenly appears in books we're reading. Strangers make comments that answer questions they don't know we're asking. Events that seem to happen by chance fit into God's plan for the education of our souls. What looks like a catastrophe is actually a burning bush from which God is speaking.[5]

As we recognize the Lord's hand at work, we will naturally pray more and interact with Him more. Although there will be obstacles in our path—we still have an enemy who does not want us to be in relationship with our Creator—this realization of God's hand in our daily lives will have the effect of drawing us closer to Him.

That's the point. Knowing the Lord is there with you in all you do. Building relationship with Him throughout the normal events of life. Drawing closer to Him in the everyday-ness of your relationship. Making God Himself and your relationship with Him the very center of all you do.

Personal application:

1. What difference would it mean for you to "tune your heart toward God"? What difference might it make today and the next day and...?

2. Write your own prayer, as John Baillie and Brother Lawrence did, that expresses to God your desire to let your worship linger all day long.

3. What type of reminder(s) might help you remember the Lord is with you in all you do? Try some of them in the next few days.

$\mathcal{E}$pilogue

$\mathcal{S}$o where does all this leave us? We've taken a lengthy look at building our lives on the foundation of God's love, which is *the* foundation for making everything else (including everything else in this book) work. We've seen the necessity of our relationship with Him and a few of the things that can be obstacles to that relationship. We have even explored some of the practical how-to's.

Allow me a few moments to leave you with some closing thoughts. My prayer is that this book will help change some of our cultural thinking and put us on a more solid, scriptural foundation.

It is vital for you to use this book not as an end in itself, but as a springboard into deepening your relationship with God. Ultimately, you will not be judged on what *I* said but on what *you* believe. The Scriptures declare that the believers in Berea were of more noble character than some others. Part of the reason given for this was because they "examined the Scriptures every day to see if what Paul said was true" (Acts 17:11). You also should continue to study and search the truth of God's eternal Word.

At the very beginning of this book we talked about priorities: what's really important. Scottish playwright James Barrie once made a powerful statement. "The life of every man is a diary in which he intends to write one story, but instead writes another. And his saddest hour is when he compares the volume as it is with what he vowed to make it."

Is God *the* most important thing in your life? Is knowing Him really the first priority of your life? He wants a close, intimate, personal relationship with you. Again, the whole point of the cross is to bring us into relationship with the Lord.

You and I desperately need a heart attitude that says, "I consider everything a loss compared to the surpassing greatness of knowing Christ Jesus my Lord" (Philippians 3:8).

As I was working on this book, I happened to be on a ministry trip to Florida. One evening I went for a walk on the beach. As I gazed out at a very small part of a very vast ocean, I thought about the wonder of knowing the God Who made all of that. He created the entire earth and all of the universe. Yet the desire of His heart is to be in relationship with us. What a privilege has been afforded us that we can know the Maker of all. It is astounding to me that we can be in relationship with God.

Make your relationship with Him *your* highest goal in life. Spend some extra time in prayer today. Take a few more minutes than usual and praise Him for His goodness toward you. Listen to His voice. Study the Scriptures and apply the truth of His Word to your life.

All the other things can wait. Seek the Lord. He promised He would be found by us when we seek Him with our whole heart. Don't put it off.

$\mathcal{N}$otes

Chapter 1

1. Dr. Donald W. McCulough, *The Trivialization of God* (Colorado Springs, Colorado: NavPress, 1995).

Chapter 2

1. Victoria Brooks, *Ministering to God* (Cedar Rapids, Iowa: Arrow Publications, 1996).

Chapter 3

1. W.E. Vine, *Vine's Expository Dictionary of New Testament Words* (Iowa Falls, Iowa: Riverside Book and Bible House).
2. Chris Fabry, *Away With the Manger: A Spiritually Correct Christmas* (Downers Grove, Illinois: InterVarsity Press, 1996).

Chapter 5

1. Dr. Gary Mathena, *One Thing Needful* (Chickasaw, Alabama: Yess Press, 1997), pgs. 2-3.

Chapter 6

1. Barnes' Notes, Electronic Database, 2 Peter 1:3. Copyright 1997 by Biblesoft.

Chapter 7

1. C.S. Lewis, *Perelandra* (New York, New York: The Macmillan Company, 1944), pg. 195.
2. Charles Swindoll, *The Grace Awakening* (Dallas, Texas: Word Publishing, 1990), pg. 44.

Chapter11

1. Max Lucado, *No Wonder They Call Him Savior* (Portland, Oregon: Multnomah Press, 1986), pg. 76.

Chapter 17

1. Bill Hull, *Building High Commitment in a Low Commitment World* (Grand Rapids, Michigan: Fleming H. Revell, 1995), pg. 41.
2. Os Guinness, *The Call* (Nashville, Tennessee: Word Publishing, 1998), pg. 175.
3. Bill Hull, *Building High Commitment in a Low Commitment World* (Grand Rapids, Michigan: Fleming H. , 1995), pg. 75.

Chapter 19

1. Jim Cymbala, *Fresh Wind, Fresh Fire* (Grand Rapids, Michigan: Zondervan Publishing House, 1997), pg. 139.

Chapter 21

1. J.I. Packer, "Foreward," in R.C. Sproul, *Knowing Scripture* (Downers Grove, Illinois: InterVarsity Press, 1979), pgs 9-10.
2. Bill Hull, *Building High Commitment in a Low Commitment World* (Grand Rapids, Michigan: H. Fleming Revell, 1995), pgs. 54-55.

Chapter 24

1. John Piper, *A Godward Life* (Sisters, Oregon: Multnomah Press, 1997), pgs. 122-123.

Chapter 27

1. Bob Sorge, *In His Face* (Canandaigua, New York: Oasis House, 1994), pg. 18.

Chapter 28

1. C.H. Spurgeon, "Peace by Believing," *Metropolitan Tabernacle Pulpit*, (London, England: Passmore and Alabaster, 1984). Reprint, Vol. 9 (Pasadena, Texas: Pilgrim Publications, 1970), pg. 283.

Chapter 29

1. John Baillie, *A Diary of Private Prayer* (New York, New York: Collier, 1977), pg. 9.
2. Brother Lawrence, *The Practice of God's Presence*, trans. Robert J. Edmonson (Orleans, Massachusetts: Paraclete Press, 1985), pg. 120.
3. Jan Johnson, *Enjoying the Presence of God* (Colorado Springs, Colorado: NavPress, 1996), pg. 19.
4. ibid, pgs. 35-36.
5. ibid, pg. 79.

About the Author

Tom Kraeuter has a heart for God and God's people. He has been face-to-face with thousands of believers from all walks of the Body of Christ, encouraging and training them to seize their full potential in the Lord Jesus Christ. A gifted communicator, Tom can articulate with spectacular clarity. People of all ages receive new insights from his straightforward, humorous style. His unpretentious passion for Jesus is infectious. A pastor from Philadelphia, Pennsylvania, said it this way, "Tom has a deep and obvious love for the Lord Jesus Christ, a passion for knowing God in a deeper way, and a wonderful ability to communicate those qualities."

Tom ministers in churches across the nation on a full-time basis through seminars, conferences, retreats, individual services, and more. These meetings are held at churches of all types and backgrounds. From Assemblies of God to Presbyterian, Baptist to Pentecostal, Vineyard to Mennonite, the response is always overwhelmingly positive.

The two main themes of Tom's teaching are worship (relationship with God) and unity (relationship with fellow believers). Although certainly not limited to these topics, in all of his teaching Tom endeavors to fulfill what he believes to be his calling from the Lord: To help as many people as possible develop a dynamic, Scripturally based relationship with God and His Church.

Presently Tom has seven other books to his credit. He is the former managing editor of *Psalmist* magazine and his writings have been featured in nationally recognized periodicals such as *Growing Churches, Ministries Today,* and *Worship Leader.*

Tom Kraeuter (pronounced Kroyter) has been a part of the leadership team of Christian Outreach Church, near St. Louis, Missouri, since 1984. He and his wife, Barbara, and their three children reside in Hillsboro, Missouri.